FORT WILLIAM
&
THE ROAD TO THE ISLES

THE GUIDE BOOK

Published in 2011
by
Aird Trading, Aird House, Aird of Sleat,
Isle of Skye. IV45 8RN.
Author: Lynne Woods
Assistant Editor: Doug Vickers
Field Assistant: Lance Jackson

ISBN 978-0-9562126-2-7

Printed by Mayoh Press Ltd.
www.mayohpress.com

Cover picture: Ben Nevis from The Caledonian Canal at Corpach

INTRODUCTION

Welcome to "Fort William & The Road To The Isles: The Guide Book," another in the series "See it...Do it....Don't miss it." The aim of each of these books is to help visitors do just that, to make the most of their stay in a given area. This part of Scotland is one of many contrasts – from the lively bustling town of Fort William and the busy fishing port of Mallaig to hauntingly beautiful places which can truly be called "remote." It would be impossible to list everything of interest or name every individual shop, hotel, gallery etc. However, what we do try to do in our guide books is to introduce you to an area and to, not only point out the well publicised sights, but to also guide you "off the beaten track" where you might not otherwise have ventured.

The book is divided into sections, arranged in a logical order for touring either part or all of the area. The numbers on the map on page 7 correspond with the numbered sections of the book. Please note that in our books the maps are not intended for precision navigation – their purpose is to illustrate the general location of those things mentioned in the text. You will notice that in this part of the World many names have more than one spelling and that there is often more than one place with the same name. It all adds to the interest!

Inside the back cover you will find a list of appropriate Ordnance Survey maps. There is also a list of useful telephone numbers. Public toilets are listed in red in most sections, where appropriate. We have also included some places where internet access is available but this is changing so rapidly that it is not possible to be totally comprehensive.

Whilst every attempt has been made to ensure accuracy, things do change with the creation of new enterprises and the disappearance of others as people retire or move on, a fact for which the publishers cannot accept responsibility.

If this is the first time you have used one of our guide books, we hope that it will enable you to make the most of your time in the area and that we may play a small part in creating some wonderful memories for you to carry home.

CONTENTS

WELCOME TO THE AREA

Throughout history, Fort William has been strategically important. At the junction of Lochs Linnhe and Eil, it forms a natural boundary between north and south. It also sits at the southern end of the Great Glen and the beginning of the route west to the Inner and Outer Hebrides. Over a hundred miles (160km) from Glasgow and nearly a hundred and fifty miles (240km) from Edinburgh, Fort William is the main town of the Western Highlands. The nearest place of any size is Inverness, some sixty -five miles (105km) away to the north east, on the opposite coast.

Fort William

Fort William is a popular tourist destination and a major centre for climbing, walking, skiing, mountain biking and a host of other outdoor pursuits – justifiably having adopted the title "The Outdoor Capital of the UK." Its geographical location ensures that, as well as having much to offer visitors, it is an excellent stepping off place for travelling further north or west.

The Scenery

It is impossible to describe the area covered by this book without using superlatives: Ben Nevis is Britain's highest mountain and Loch Morar its deepest inland stretch of water. The construction of The Caledonian Canal was, at the time, one of the World's greatest engineering triumphs and the beautiful "Road to The Isles," whether travelled by road or The West Highland Railway, is listed among the World's most scenic journeys.

Glen Nevis

The Wildlife

A huge variety of natural habitats exist in this wild and unspoilt corner of Britain. Many creatures elsewhere considered rare or exotic are here almost commonplace. Golden eagles and other birds of prey soar above

A colony of seals

the mountains, while elusive game birds such as ptarmigan and capercaillie nest lower on the moors: The seas are home to otters, dolphins, porpoises, seals and whales, while in the forests and rivers which lie between mountain and sea live pine martens, red squirrels and a host of other creatures.

The History
The area is steeped in Clan history with romantic tales of battles and heroic deeds. There has been mass rebellion against outside influence and also great poverty and hardship at the hands of landlords, even to the point of forced emigration. The most well known historical figure, however, is no doubt that of Charles Edward Stuart, Bonnie Prince Charlie. His eighteenth century bid to take the throne saw him roaming much of the area, gathering his supporters and subsequently, after defeat at Culloden, making his escape across the wild country of the Western Highlands.

Something for everyone....
Fort William, the surrounding area and the Road To The Isles really does have something for everyone and can cater for all tastes (and energy levels!) From an action packed activity holiday to an interest-filled history trail or simply a relaxing getaway amongst stunning scenery, there is space for everyone to enjoy this beautiful part of Scotland in their own way....

Something for everyone....

Please note: Petrol stations can be few and far between in some areas.

CHARLES EDWARD STUART: BONNIE PRINCE CHARLIE

Born in Rome in 1720, Charles was the son of James "The Old Pretender" and grandson of James VII of Scotland and II of England. He was landed on mainland Scotland by a French ship in August 1745 to regain the throne for The House of Stewart.* After raising his father's royal standard at Glenfinnan, he gathered a Highland army about him and marched on Edinburgh which was taken without difficulty. A subsequent victory over Government troops at the Battle of Prestonpans was followed by a march south into England which saw the Jacobite army occupy Carlisle, Lancaster, Preston and Manchester in turn before gaining possession of Derby. However, after much disagreement between Charles and his senior commanders, a retreat was ordered and the Scots retraced their steps to Scotland whereupon Charles engaged in a further battle at Falkirk. Again he was victorious but failed to follow up his success by retaking Edinburgh and withdrew further north to Inverness. There, on the 16th June 1746 at Culloden, his Jacobites met the government army led by the Duke of Cumberland. Charles was decisively beaten and made his escape through the Highlands to the Western Isles, taking shelter with various supporters, most notable of whom was Flora MacDonald who was instrumental in the Prince successfully evading capture. Later this brave lady was imprisoned by the government for her activities. She was perhaps more fortunate than many of her contemporaries who paid with their lives in the hunt for Charles and his Jacobites in the days and weeks following the battle. Eventually Charles was able to take a French ship and left Scotland never to return. A saddened and less spirited man, he lived out his days in France and Italy, dying in 1788.

Inscription on The Prince's Cairn,

* Confusingly, common usage has evolved as "Stuart" when referring to the Prince but "Stewart" when referring to The House of Stewart.

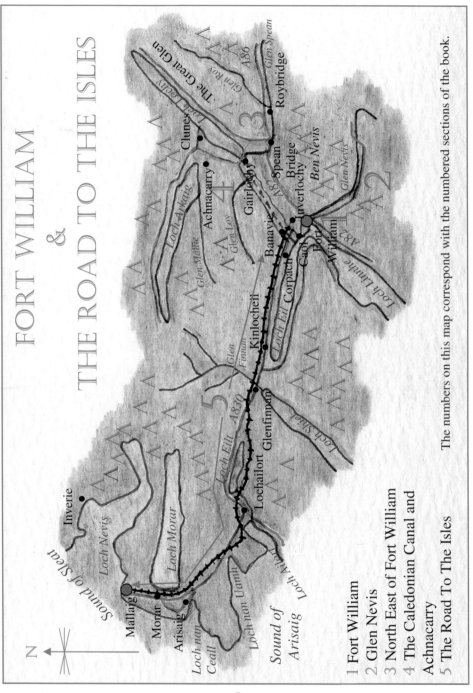

FORT WILLIAM
&
THE ROAD TO THE ISLES

N

The numbers on this map correspond with the numbered sections of the book.

1 Fort William
2 Glen Nevis
3 North East of Fort William
4 The Caledonian Canal and
Achnacarry
5 The Road To The Isles

FORT WILLIAM

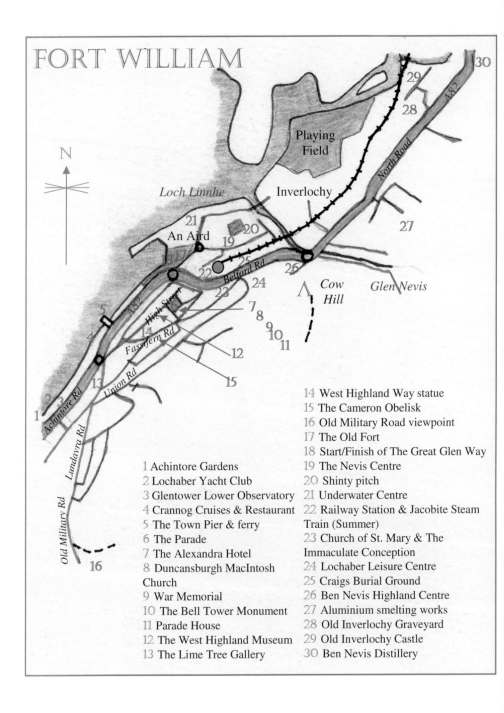

Playing Field

Loch Linnhe

Inverlochy

An Aird

Cow Hill

Glen Nevis

14 West Highland Way statue
15 The Cameron Obelisk
16 Old Military Road viewpoint
17 The Old Fort
18 Start/Finish of The Great Glen Way
1 Achintore Gardens
2 Lochaber Yacht Club
3 Glentower Lower Observatory
4 Crannog Cruises & Restaurant
5 The Town Pier & ferry
6 The Parade
7 The Alexandra Hotel
8 Duncansburgh MacIntosh Church
9 War Memorial
10 The Bell Tower Monument
11 Parade House
12 The West Highland Museum
13 The Lime Tree Gallery
19 The Nevis Centre
20 Shinty pitch
21 Underwater Centre
22 Railway Station & Jacobite Steam Train (Summer)
23 Church of St. Mary & The Immaculate Conception
24 Lochaber Leisure Centre
25 Craigs Burial Ground
26 Ben Nevis Highland Centre
27 Aluminium smelting works
28 Old Inverlochy Graveyard
29 Old Inverlochy Castle
30 Ben Nevis Distillery

1   FORT WILLIAM

Fort William (Gaelic: An Gearasdan, translated literally as "The Garrison,") has a long and eventful history, not all of it peaceful. Nestling beneath the mighty Ben Nevis, Britain's highest mountain, the town has undergone several name changes, although every reference book seems to contain a different version. In times of Clan dominance, the whole area was Cameron country. The Highlands were considered by the Crown to be lawless and unruly and in 1654 a fort was built here to house Cromwell's troops. Built by General Monk, it was constructed of earth and wood but was extended and rebuilt in stone in 1690 by order of William III and called Fort William. A village grew up around the fort, initially called Maryburgh after William's queen but at various later times also known as Gordonsburgh and Duncansburgh.

It was from here that troops marched out to Glencoe in 1692, prior to the infamous Glencoe Massacre. Twice, in 1715 and 1746, the fort was besieged by the Jacobites but on both occasions managed to withstand. Some damage was sustained in the latter siege and the fort was subsequently reinforced and extended by order of Prince William, Duke of Cumberland (later nicknamed "Butcher Cumberland.") The fort and village together were then known as Fort William.

Fort William on the shores of Loch Linnhe

Throughout the eighteenth century the town steadily grew as a cattle and sheep trading centre. By the 1820's a regular steam boat service from Glasgow carried early tourists as well as goods and in 1822 the Caledonian Canal opened, linking Fort William with Inverness. This established a through route from Glasgow to Inverness.

In 1873 Queen Victoria visited the town. Then in 1894 the railway arrived, an event which sealed its future as a tourist centre. Walkers, climbers, fishermen and writers were all drawn to the town, along with the less energetic but affluent classes as travel became fashionable. A further move into the "modern age" came later the same decade when, in 1896, the town became the first place in Britain to be lit by hydro-electric power. This was supplied by the "Fort William Electric Lighting Company." The hydro-electric scheme was considerably extended thirty years later to provide power for an aluminium smelting plant, an industry which continues today.

WWII saw Fort William as a naval training centre, HMS. St. Christopher being the name of the base. Between 1940 and 1944 some fifty thousand men completed short courses here.

Over the years the fort had gradually fallen into disrepair. At one time the site was used as an engine shed and marshalling yard by the West Highland Railway who demolished the last of the fort buildings in 1948, although some remains can still be

FORT WILLIAM (CONT'D)

seen on the seaward side of the road.

During the 1950's came yet another move to change the town's name: The name Abernevis was suggested but was resisted.

As a natural hub for road, rail and water transport, the town has developed into a place which caters for locals and tourists alike. It has supermarkets, some of the usual high street chains and a large number of souvenir outlets, cafés, restaurants and take-aways. The town can offer a wide choice of outdoor pursuits and abundant accommodation from backpacking hostels to hotels. Each July Fort William holds its annual Highland Games. Modern Fort William is a lively and bustling town, one in which most visitors to the north of Scotland or the west coast find themselves at some stage.

BEN NEVIS

Ben Nevis, the anglicized version of the Gaelic "Beinn Nibheis," translates as "mountain touching the clouds," although an alternative version suggests "venomous mountain." At 4406' (1342m) "The Ben," to use its affectionate abbreviation, is Britain's highest mountain but it can sometimes be a slight disappointment because its full majesty is disguised on either side by being joined to a range of slightly lower, but still impressive peaks. Two of these lie within a mile (1.5km) of the main summit, giving the effect that the three are indeed but one mountain. The true glory of Ben Nevis can only really be appreciated from the summit, a small plateau flanked by gigantic cliffs on two sides.

During the nineteenth century, scientific interest in meteorology and the atmosphere meant that data obtained from high levels was invaluable for furthering knowledge. On the summit of Ben Nevis are the remains of an observatory built in 1883 and in use until 1904 taking readings every single hour. A track had to be built for ponies to first carry up building materials and then, later, supplies for the two observers and the cook who lived there. Conditions in winter were extremely harsh and the men were often cut off for months at a time.

From the summit, on a clear day the views over much of the Highlands are spectacular but the mountain is often wreathed in mist. Keats, the poet, obviously found it so: Reaching the summit in 1819 he was moved to write a sonnet in which the word "mist" appears several times and is referred to as a "shroud."

The Ben Nevis summit, along with the summits of Carn Mor Dearg, Aonach Beag and Sgurr Choinnich Beag, is owned by the John Muir Trust which works with the Nevis Partnership to bring together all interested parties in the area to care for the land – no mean task when over a hundred thousand people climb to the top of "The Ben" each year.

(For more details on climbing Ben Nevis see the Glen Nevis section.)

10

The Sea Front

Although a busy dual carriageway runs along the front, the views across Loch Linnhe more than make up for the sound

Loch Linnhe

of traffic. Approaching the town from the south the road is lined with the many hotels and guest houses which enjoy this superb outlook and there is a large car park near to the attractive sea front **Achintore Gardens.** A reddy, pink building also south of the town centre, on the A82, is the former **Glentower Lower Observatory.** Built in 1889 to provide readings to compare with those taken from the summit of Ben Nevis, the lower observatory contained self recording instruments which were used between 1890 and 1904. A Grade B Listed building, it is now an elegant B and B. The recordings, log books and data sheets are held in the Edinburgh Meteorological Office. A book "The Weathermen of Ben Nevis" by Margaret Roy tells the fascinating story of the men who worked here and at the observatory on the summit of Ben Nevis.

Lochaber Yacht Club. The sailing club welcomes visiting boats. There is a visitor's mooring near the club and additional ones are usually available run by Achintore Moorings Association. Water is available at the club house and diesel at the Caledonian Canal basin.

The Town Pier. Departing from here, "Souter's Lass" is a sturdy pleasure cruiser which retains many of her original 1948 features. Operated by **Crannog Cruises**, she can now boast the addition of some modern facilities including toilets, a bar and lounge serving drinks and snacks and a covered viewing area. The skipper's commentary is lively and informative and this is a relaxing way to gain some of the best views of Fort William and Ben Nevis, as well as the chance to do some wildlife spotting: Seals, otters and porpoises are common in these waters. Evening cruises are also available during the summer months.

The Crannog Restaurant

The Crannog Restaurant

For a truly gastronomic experience Fort William's seafood restaurant, perched on the stone pier jutting into Loch Linnhe, is a must. An all-year round menu features imaginative flavour combinations, daily specials depending on the local catch. Open 12.00 - 2.30, 6pm – 9pm, daily except Xmas Day, Boxing Day, New Year's Day and the evenings of Dec. 24th and 31st. Booking is essential. Seafood can also be purchased direct from the **Crannog Seafood Company.** www.crannog.net

Camusnagaul Bay

Also departing from the town pier, several times daily Mon. – Sat. throughout the year, is the small ferry which crosses Loch

The Camusnagaul Ferry, Town Pier

Linnhe to this pretty bay. Among 66 hectares of community-owned ancient oakwood is **"The Crofters' Walk,"** a way marked trail. As well as the chance to spot red squirrels, roe deer and some unusual moths (including the rare Chequered Skipper moth) two pollarded oak trees can be found in the woods. "Pollarding" is a method of pruning the trunk and main branches so that side shoots form to give a bushy effect. At one time the bark would be soaked in water for use in tanning, while the timber would be made into charcoal. It is interesting to note that one of the possible reasons for the Chequered Skipper moth becoming extinct in England was the fact that large scale coppicing was no longer common –

coppicing employs a similar technique to pollarding but at the base of tree. During the summer months tea and home-made cakes are usually for sale at nearby **Trislaig Village Hall** .

The Parade

The Parade

At the top end of the High Street is The Parade, once the fort parade ground and now a pleasant open space surrounded by some imposing buildings and home to several interesting monuments and memorials.

The Alexandra Hotel has dominated the Parade area since 1876 and is a typical Victorian hotel. Facilities include **The Food Stop** – a modern restaurant to the side of the hotel serving food from 10am to 9.30pm daily during the summer months, reduced hours out of season.

Duncansburgh MacIntosh Church. Sir Duncan Cameron of Fassifern donated generously towards the cost of the church. In gratitude the parishioners attempted to have the town renamed Duncansburgh but only the church retains the name. A grade B listed building, it is an impressive structure with an attractive buttressed tower. The date 1881 is carved over the doorway, although it was the following year when the church was completed. In 2007 the congregation of the MacIntosh

The Duncansburgh MacIntosh Church

Memorial Church joined with that of the Duncansburgh, hence its present name.
In front of the church stands The **War Memorial**: On top stands a statue of a soldier in a kilt, his head bowed.

Donald Cameron Of Lochiel

Adjacent to the War Memorial is a **bronze statue of Donald Cameron of Lochiel**, twenty - fourth chief of Clan Cameron. The statue is by W. Birnie Rhind and dates from 1909 when it was "erected by clansmen and friends in token of their devotion, respect and admiration." The inscription is in both English and Gaelic. As well as Chief, he was Lord Lieutenant of Inverness-shire for many years and represented the county in parliament. He was an early advocate of the West Highland Railway and was also involved in the Napier Commission which established the rights of crofters.

The Bell Tower is a fascinating civic monument. The bell housing came from the former town hall in Cameron Square, a building dating from 1790 which originally served as Maryburgh Church.

The Bell Tower Monument

The bell was rescued after the building burned down in 1975. The plinth is of granite salvaged from the fort. The monument celebrates the friendship between Hiroshima, Dudley and Fort William and a similar piece of granite from Fort William can be seen in Hiroshima's Peace Park. The monument invokes youth from across the world to work together for peace.

The Governor's House, originally called **Parade House** and now the offices of Scottish National Heritage, was built around 1772 to house the Governor of the fort. It was one of the town's first stone buildings - prior to this all buildings outside the fort were of timber so the Governor could order them to be burned if there was trouble in the town.

13

The High Street

The High Street dates from the 1830's when Sir Duncan Cameron of Fassifern instigated many improvements to the town. Nowadays it is a pedestrianised shopping street with the usual banks, post office, pharmacies etc. There are also several bars and restaurants and a large number of specialist shops selling outdoor clothing and equipment, souvenirs and Scottish products to suit all budgets.

Nevisport

Nevisport

At one end of the High Street, the shop is identified by the gondola cabin suspended outside. This is on the site of the former hanging tree where the town's miscreants met their end! The shop sells a wide range of branded outdoor clothing, footwear and equipment. Staff are knowledgeable and helpful. Upstairs is a good selection of books and maps and a café.

Ian Wynne & Son, Butchers, is a must for anyone self catering. As well as a huge choice of best quality meat, they produce their own haggis, black puddings, fruit puddings and yummy steak pies – all made on the premises.

Crofters Bar & Restaurant is a lively public house at the western end of the High Street and a good place to watch live televised sport.

St. Andrew's Episcopal Church

Consecrated in 1880, St. Andrew's replaced an earlier church from 1817 which was known as the Rosse Chapel after the Countess of Ross. (Again, the difference in spelling is not a mistake!) When this fell into disrepair George Baynton Davy paid for its demolition and much of the cost of erecting the present church. It was designed by Inverness architect Alexander Ross and is built of granite from Abriachan on the western side of Loch Ness. The interior wood carving is by Harry Hems of Exeter, as are the grand oak outer doors. The church baptistery has a beautiful Italian mosaic floor.

St. Andrew's Episcopal Church

Bank Street Lodge offers good value hostel type accommodation with a self catering kitchen. Adjacent to the hostel is **The Stables Restaurant** serving a variety of food and catering for groups if booked in advance.

The Rod & Gun Shop

This well stocked shop sells most requirements for freshwater and sea

14

fishing as well as shooting. It is also the place for knowledgeable advice and permits for fishing throughout the area. **The Café Chardon** just off the High Street sells freshly made sandwiches, baguettes and pastries to eat in or take away.

The Highland Woollen Company is one of two Edinburgh Woollen Mill outlets selling an extensive range of reasonably priced clothing.

The Maryburgh Inn. Situated through some narrow, cast iron gates which lead down some steps from the High Street, this is a traditional Scottish pub.

The Maryburgh Inn

VisitScotland Information Centre
As well as selling a range of maps and guide books, VisitScotland staff are pleased to make bookings and provide advice and information.

Café Mango
Serving both Thai and Indian cuisine, it is refreshing to find an ethnic restaurant where the dishes are all home made with fresh ingredients. Open 12 – 10 pm daily.

Cameron Square
The square is named after the volunteer regiment raised here in 1793 which, in 1873, became the Queen's Own Cameron Highlanders. (Queen Victoria.) These valiant men are also remembered in the

name of the public house at the bottom of the square.

The Volunteer Arms

The Volunteer Arms

Known as "The Volley," this is one of Fort William's oldest public houses, dating from around 1871 although the date above the door (1925) commemorates its re-opening after a major refurbishment. Its name honours the volunteers of the Cameron Highlanders. Around the bar is a collection of old photographs. There is live entertainment throughout the summer. Thursdays and Sundays are especially popular when there is traditional Scottish music.

The Nevis Bakery is a great place to buy picnic food, having won awards for its savoury baking.

No 4 Restaurant
The emphasis here is definitely on the best of Scottish cuisine – dishes, including desserts, are all prepared on the premises from locally sourced ingredients. A favourite starter is local haggis with whisky sauce and the café has a reputation for serving quality local venison.

The West Highland Museum
Founded in 1922 and housed in what was The British Linen Bank in Cameron

Square, this is a true gem. What makes this independent museum special is a refreshing lack of high tech gimmickry which leaves visitors free to admire some fascinating artefacts, including those in its world famous Jacobite collection. One intriguing exhibit is a "secret portrait" of Bonnie Prince Charlie – a semicircle of apparently random splodges until viewed as a reflection on a shiny cylinder. Also on view is a mail bag fashioned from a sheep's stomach and used by inhabitants of St. Kilda to send mail to the Isle of

The West Highland Museum

Lewis by throwing the bag into the sea! Another exhibit is a gruesome birching table with its strap holes, last used in 1948. Other sections include the landscape, wildlife, weaponry, regiments, coinage, social history, maps – something to interest everyone. The museum gift shop has a range of unusual books, prints and old fashioned toys.

The High Street C'td

The House of Scotland: Suppliers of all things tartan from lengths of fabric to full Highland dress, sporrans, Celtic jewellery, clan products and a huge range of Scottish giftware.

The Highland Soap Company

Hand made soaps

A place of true temptation! The company has a complete range of hand made cosmetic products which are entirely natural and made just up the road at Spean Bridge, using the centuries old "cold process."

The Grog and Gruel

The Grog and Gruel

Half way along the pedestrian precinct, this is a popular pub serving a good range of real ales and around sixty different malt whiskies. The menu is a reasonably priced, imaginative, cross-culture mix available from 12.00 to 9pm every day in the bar or the upstairs restaurant. This is also the place to obtain the final stamp in the West Highland Way Log Book scheme. Open all year round except Sundays in deepest, darkest winter. Free WiFi access.

Ben Nevis Book Corner

The Ben Nevis Book Corner

This aptly named establishment, tucked away in Monzie Square, is a real find for book addicts. Although small, there is a vast selection of second hand books, many of them rare or out of print.

The Whisky Shop

This is one of a Scottish chain of specialist shops, founded in 1992 and now with

The Whisky Shop

branches throughout the length and breadth of the country. There is a huge range of whiskies in stock and plenty of advice on hand from staff.

The Highland Camera Company (Redcat Scotland) - as the name suggests, the place to go for all things photographic. **The Tavern** is a licensed café which is

open daily until 9.30pm.

The Granite House

The shop describes itself, justifiably, as a "giftmongers" and this truly is a remarkable shop for the sheer variety and quantity of quality contemporary gifts under one roof. A past winner of "Scottish Gift Shop of The Year," there are two storeys to browse - so plan not to rush!

The Ben Nevis Bar

Centrally situated along the High Street, the Ben Nevis Bar has stood here since

The Ben Nevis Bar

1806. With two bars, open fires and serving fresh food, it is a welcoming place to stop off. Food served from 12 noon – 10pm.

CAFE 115

Serving homemade "modern Scottish" food, this licensed café/restaurant is open 9am - 9.30pm, March – October.

Alpine Bikes

Open daily in summer, Mon-Sat in winter. For mountain bike hire there are branches both in the High Street and, from May to September, at the foot of the Nevis Range.

The House of Clan Jamfrie

An extensive and imaginative selection of Scottish products, books, gifts and jewellery can be found here. This is one of those shops to enjoy a really good potter around.

Sugar & Spice

A café with an arty twist - delicious coffee and home-baking, soups and hot snacks, served in a friendly atmosphere amidst local artists' work. Fair Trade gift shop and internet access.

The Hot Roast Company

This small café/takeaway advertises itself

by the wonderful, nose-tickling aroma of roasting meat which drifts out on to the High Street. Generous slices of sizzling, freshly roasted meat are served on rolls or as plated meals. And to finish off? As well

The Hot Roast Company

as a genuinely good range of teas and coffees, if you still have room there is a choice of cakes and pastries.

The Imperial Hotel

Centrally situated and with good views over Loch Linnhe, the restaurant and bar are open to non residents all year round.

The Lime Tree Gallery

(By the roundabout on the main road at the end of the High Street.) For "somewhere with a difference" this superb, award winning restaurant also features an independent art gallery, showcasing works from national art collections as well that of local artists. Dinner 6.30pm to 9.30pm daily. Booking necessary. 01397 701806

THE WEST HIGHLAND WAY & THE GREAT GLEN WAY

Fort William is the end of this 96 mile (154 km) walk from Milngavie on the northern outskirts of Glasgow. In 2010 the official finishing point was changed to Gordon Square and is now marked by a life-sized figure of a walker sitting on a bench. However, those wishing to gain the final stamp for their log book must then walk back to the Grog and Gruel.

The Great Glen Way

The official start (or finish) of the 73 mile (117km) walk between Fort William and Inverness, known as The Great Glen Way, is marked by a plaque and information board on the grassed area near the old fort. For those with neither time nor energy to walk 73 miles, the board is still worth a visit if only for the aerial photograph of the Great Glen!

Behind the High Street

Tucked away among the residential streets behind the High Street are some interesting buildings and monuments:

The Highland Hotel

Commanding panoramic views over the town, The Highland Hotel on Union Road is an impressive Victorian building with a cast iron balcony, typical of the era. It has an interesting history: The fact that it was originally called The Station Hotel, although nowhere near the station, bears testimony to the political wrangling which was common between railway companies and developers during the latter part of the nineteenth century. The hotel was sold and given its present name in 1910 - for many years providing educational holidays for students from London's Regent Park College. It then saw an interlude as a

The Highland Hotel

training school for military amputees learning to cut and polish diamonds. During WWII it became part of HMS Christopher, the shore based naval training centre and it has since belonged to various tour companies and has been bankrupt more than once. However, it is now enjoying happier days: Fully refurbished, it once again provides a high standard of accommodation, mostly for coach parties but also catering for independent travellers.

Cameron Obelisk

Cameron Obelisk

On Fassifern Road, in a small garden, stands an obelisk in memory of Captain Peter Cameron (1777 – 1843.) The structure was erected by "His attached brother Sir Duncan Cameron, of Fassfern Baronet, in the year 1847." (The difference in the spelling of Fassfern here is not a printing error!)

Old Military Road Viewpoint

Lundavra Road leads steeply out of the town to Old Military Road. The viewpoint, with picnic benches and a

Old Military Road Viewpoint

telescope, is at the summit of the hill, about a mile (1.5km) from the town centre. The road eventually tapers out at Lochan Lunn Da Bhrà. A track from just below the viewpoint leads to Cow Hill.

An Aird

An Aird, signposted from Morrison's roundabout, is the area where the Rivers Lochy and Nevis join Loch Linnhe.

The Fort (An Gearasdan)

Remains of The Old Fort

The former fort area is a pleasant, grassed open space on the sea front. Some of the ramparts remain and it is in an interesting place to explore with information boards about the area's history. A further part of the fort survives elsewhere – an arched gateway, dating from the seventeenth century, was removed and re-erected in the Craig's Burial Ground on the A82, just north of the hospital..

Underwater Centre

Not an aquarium, this is a dive centre offering equipment hire, charter boats, guided dives and accredited training.

The Nevis Centre

This is a popular venue for live entertainment and other events as well as housing a Superbowl, café and facilities for playing table tennis, pool, badminton etc. Open 12.00 – 10.00pm. daily except Christmas Day, Boxing Day and January 1st – 2nd.

Shinty Club

An Aird is the home ground of Fort William Shinty Club, one of Scotland's top teams and known simply as "The Fort." Shinty is a team game, not entirely dissimilar to hockey and played almost exclusively in Scotland.

There is also a **McDonald's** restaurant at An Aird.

Belford Road

This is the A82 between the two roundabouts at Morrisons and Nevis Bridge. An underpass leads from the station end of the High Street to **Fort William Railway Station** and **Morrisons supermarket.**

The Railway Station

The Lochaber Café is situated in the station concourse and serves meals all day. There is also a travel centre for **Caledonian MacBrayne** and **a travel agent. Bill's Place** is a well stocked news-stand selling papers, magazines, guide books etc. and, for train enthusiasts, this is the place for a close encounter with a **steam locomotive – The Jacobite** departs from here on summer mornings. It is also where the nightly sleeper train leaves for London. The **Bus Station** is adjacent to the train station.

The Church of St. Mary and The Immaculate Conception

Beyond the hospital, this grade A listed building was created by architect Reginald Fairlie and completed in 1934. Fairlie was responsible for a number of West Highland Catholic churches and this one is typical of his style – the outside impressively solid with strong lines, the interior beautifully simple.

Craigs Burial Ground

On the A82 north, opposite Lochaber Leisure Centre, this burial ground was originally the cemetery for the fort and is full of fascinating gravestones and memorials. The large classical archway was the main entrance to the fort, re-

The Archway from The Original Fort

erected here in 1896. It spans the line of General Wade's original military road. An inscription reads:

This arch was erected in 1690 over the main entrance to the fort and re-erected here in 1896 where Sir Allan Cameron of Erracht in 1793 raised the 79th or Cameron Highlanders, a regiment which distinguished itself on many a hard fought field for king and country.

Craig's Burial Ground

One memorial is to men who fought in the South African War of 1899 – 1902. There is also a large obelisk dedicated to Ewan MacLachlan (1775 – 1822) who is considered to have played a crucial role in the preservation of the Gaelic language. As well as writing Gaelic verse he translated much ancient classical literature into Gaelic.

Lochaber Leisure Centre

Open daily, facilities include a 25m swimming pool, gym, sauna, squash courts etc.

The Ben Nevis Highland Centre

This is a large retail centre selling clothing and Scottish themed gifts and souvenirs. There is a specialist whisky section and a clan tartan centre as well as a restaurant and ample parking.

The Nevis Bank Inn offers comfortable accommodation at the western end of the town near the entrance to Glen Nevis. Browns Restaurant and Bar has a varied menu using locally sourced food. Open all year round – the winter warmer lunch offers good value in nice surroundings.

Inverlochy.

Prior to there being a fort, in the 1600's Inverlochy was the only settlement. "Modern" Inverlochy is a garden suburb village, purpose built in the 1920's to house workers from the new smelter of the British Aluminium Company. Inverlochy is most visited for its castle on the banks of the **River Lochy** which flows into Loch Linnhe after its nine mile (14km) journey from Loch Lochy. During WWII the river saw tragedy when twelve commandos drowned during training.

HYDRO-ELECTRIC POWER AND THE ALUMINIUM INDUSTRY

Dominating the mountain Meall an t-Suidhe behind Fort William are the great pipes which run down the mountain as part of an enormous hydro-electric power scheme. It was established during the 1920's by the then Grampian Electricity Company to provide sufficient electricity for the aluminium works. A fifteen mile (24km) long tunnel was bored through the mountain to carry water from Loch Treig and Loch Laggan. At the time it was the biggest tunnelling project in the World. During construction, the line of the railway track had to be raised thirty feet (9m) to accommodate Loch Treig's greater depth when its water was joined with the flow from Loch Laggan. As with any modern day development, there was much concern over possible environmental effects, as expressed by contemporary author *[1] J.J. Bell:

"The River Treig, which used to pour from the northern end to join the Spean, was a mere trickle when I saw it lately, its bed obscenely exposed. And the splendid Spean itself – what of its trout and salmon in the future? But man must be served."

There is still an aluminium smelter on the outskirts of the town. The company, no longer British Aluminium, is Australian based and is a major employer in the town. The molten metal is cast into ingots which are transported elsewhere to be transformed into tinfoil and car parts etc.

Huge pipes running down the side of the mountain behind the town

*[1] The Glory of Scotland by J.J. Bell.

Old Inverlochy Castle

The castle is signposted "Old Inverlochy Castle" to avoid confusion with a much grander and later castle which is now a luxury hotel. The former was built around 1280 by the Comyn family but (as is the way with castles!) it changed hands several times - usually by force. The Comyns lost it to supporters of Robert The Bruce. Later the castle played an important role in the two Battles of Inverlochy, in 1431 and 1645 respectively. In the latter, the Campbells were defeated

Old Inverlochy Castle

by the Marquis of Montrose, a bloody victory when over a thousand Campbells were killed in the castle grounds. Much of Inverlochy Castle remains intact and information boards show how it would have looked when inhabited.
Nevis Cycles is to be found in Inverlochy. During the summer they also have a branch called Witch's Trail Bike Hire on the approach road to the Nevis Range. Their website www.neviscycles.com has a useful link to a five day local weather forecast.

Old Inverlochy Graveyard

Old Inverlochy Graveyard

Near to the castle is this fascinating graveyard. Sadly, sheep are allowed to graze here but it is still of interest with some very old gravestones with quaint inscriptions.

The Ben Nevis Distillery

The romance which surrounds the production of "uisge beatha" or "the water of life" as Scotch whisky is known, is much in evidence at the Ben Nevis Distillery. Founded in 1825 by "Long John" Macdonald, the distillery was run by the Macdonald family for over a hundred years before passing to Joseph

The Ben Nevis Distillery

Hobbs. In 1978 production temporarily ceased. The premises were eventually taken over by Whitbread, mainly for storage, but in 1984 it was decided to re open the production plant. Five years later

The Still Room, The Ben Nevis Distillery

the company was bought by a Japanese distilling company, Nikka.
Although only eight production staff are employed, thirty five thousand visitors a year are welcomed to the visitor centre and can experience that wonderful still room smell, learn about whisky production from an excellent audio visual presentation and sample the "Dew of Ben Nevis" – for, as well as producing raw spirit for Japanese distilleries, a limited

FORT WILLIAM (CONT'D)

amount of a rather special 10 year old single malt is produced here. The taste is creamy smooth with just a hint of peat. Definitely recommended! The visitor centre has a fascinating exhibition as well as a coffee shop serving some tasty baking. Open all year Mon – Fri. plus weekends in the summer months.

Day Trips from Fort William

A wide range of day trips by train, coach and boat are possible from Fort William – too many to include a comprehensive list here. The VisitScotland Information Centre in the High Street will have full details of what is available.

M.V. Lady Gail

Fishing trips on Loch Linnhe with tackle available for hire and an experienced skipper who knows the best places to fish. Lady Gail can take up to twelve people and provides complimentary hot drinks. Tel: 01397 701567. Mobile. 07747 680498.

Caledonian MacBrayne operate day trips by coach and ferry to several of the islands and operate a **tour shop** at the station for information and bookings.

THE JACOBITE STEAM TRAIN

Running daily from mid May to Mid October between Fort William and Mallaig, this is one of the "Great Railway Journeys of The World." The scenery grows ever more spectacular with each passing mile. Views back to Ben Nevis give way to a glimpse of the eight-high flight of locks which is Neptune's Staircase. Along the shores of Loch Eil the train continues to the head of Loch Shiel and the mighty Glenfinnan Viaduct, now so familiar through the Harry Potter films. At historic Glenfinnan Station there is time to disembark and enjoy the small museum or a drink in the Station Dining Car before rejoining the train. The journey continues beneath towering mountains, over rushing streams, beneath impressive waterfalls until the sea is glimpsed once more and the Sound of Arisaig

comes into view. Beyond are the islands of Eigg and Rum and then Skye. On arriving in Mallaig there is time to explore this lively fishing port and to sample some fresh fish or even arrange to have some Mallaig kippers posted home before making the return journey to Fort William. Operates Monday to Friday mid May – mid Oct. Weekends – high season only.

24

THE WEST HIGHLAND RAILWAY

Whilst Telford's roads provided long needed access to some of the most remote areas of Western Scotland during the early part of the nineteenth century, it was the arrival of the railway almost ninety years later that opened up the area to tourists. The line between Glasgow and Fort William was completed in 1894 but the final forty-one mile (66km) leg to Mallaig was only agreed after much dispute between various railway companies: An act of parliament approving the construction of the line, as well as a harbour at Mallaig, was eventually passed and the line opened in April 1901. It is an awe inspiring piece of engineering with a total of eleven tunnels, many cuttings hewn out of solid rock and a number of elegant viaducts which are made from concrete, at that time a revolutionary idea. The bridge at Borrodale was at one time the largest concrete bridge in the world. During WWII the entire area to the west of Fort William became a special training area and access was restricted. The railway was very busy during this period transporting men and equipment, as well as carrying timber: Much wood needed for the War effort came from here.

Mallaig - The end of the line

Fort William Pier

Fort William Public Toilets
Station Square
Fort William Railway Station
Viewforth car park adjacent to Bank Street
The Nevis Centre, An Aird

Internet access
The Grog and Gruel pub
Sugar & Spice, High Street
Fort William Library.

WiFi Hotspots
The High Street near Bank Street.

25

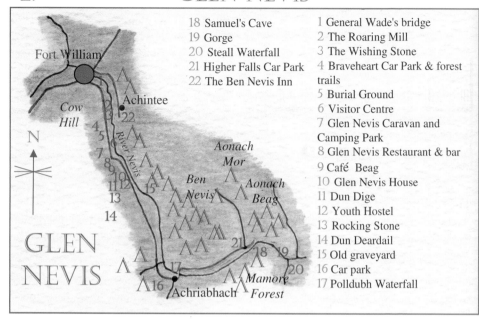

18 Samuel's Cave
19 Gorge
20 Steall Waterfall
21 Higher Falls Car Park
22 The Ben Nevis Inn

1 General Wade's bridge
2 The Roaring Mill
3 The Wishing Stone
4 Braveheart Car Park & forest trails
5 Burial Ground
6 Visitor Centre
7 Glen Nevis Caravan and Camping Park
8 Glen Nevis Restaurant & bar
9 Café Beag
10 Glen Nevis House
11 Dun Dige
12 Youth Hostel
13 Rocking Stone
14 Dun Deardail
15 Old graveyard
16 Car park
17 Polldubh Waterfall

Glen Nevis (Gaelic: "Gleann Nibheis") is one of Scotland's most picturesque glens and possibly one of the most well known because of its accessibility. The road along its length was built to provide employment during the potato famine of 1846. The glen is a deep, U shaped valley which was scoured out by massive glaciers during the ice age. Its steep, scree-covered sides rise majestically towards the sky, dominated by Ben Nevis on the eastern side and the Mamore Range to the south. Along the floor of the glen the River Nevis rushes between banks lined with alder and ash and native woodlands of oak, birch and pine trees. The latter are home to red squirrels. In the fields, Highland cattle graze peacefully, a tourist attraction in their own right!

Many tributaries carry water down the mountains to feed the river, causing the level to rise and fall considerably and it is thus termed a "spate river." At the head of the glen, beyond the road, is a beautiful gorge which opens onto meadows below a hanging valley from which tumbles the dramatic Steall Waterfall.

Historically, Glen Nevis was a stronghold of one of the five branches of Clan Cameron. The Glen Nevis Estate is owned by Camerons, as it has been since 1536. It is a hill farming estate but is managed for the benefit of visitors, with ecology, wildlife and conservation as prime concerns. The result is a sympathetic blend of tradition, recreational facilities and nature. As well as being the departure point for climbing Ben Nevis, there are plenty of lower level and less energetic walks. For the super-energetic Glen Nevis is a particularly welcome sight as the last leg of the West Highland Way.

The River Nevis

The Old Bridge of Nevis

A few hundred yards along the Glen road, on the left, can be seen one of General Wade's bridges, now only used by pedestrians. From 1724 General Wade embarked on an ambitious project to build roads and bridges throughout the Highlands in order to make it easier for government troops to keep the rebellious Scots under control. A little further along is a pool known as **The Roaring Mill** because of the noise made by the water as it is forced through a narrow gap in the rock.

The Wishing Stone

Beyond the Roaring Mill, on the footpath next to the road, is a large rock. It is a glacial erratic - a boulder carried and dumped by a glacier. However, it is surrounded by legend: A plaque declares it to be the Wishing Stone although it was traditionally known as **Samuel's Stone.** One myth is that a wish will be granted to anyone who can make the stone turn round three times; another grants the wish to anyone who sees the stone move and a further variation is that the stone can offer counsel to anyone seeking advice - but only if the question is asked while the stone is turning!

Filming in the glen

Because of its grandeur and accessibility, Glen Nevis has been used on several occasions as a film location. "Braveheart," starring Mel Gibson, was filmed here, as was "Rob Roy," "Highlander" and scenes from some of the early Harry Potter films. For the former an entire fort was constructed in the glen as well as a bridge, both of which were later removed as a condition of planning consent.

The Braveheart Car Park & Forest Trails

"Braveheart," set in the fourteenth century, tells the story of William Wallace and Scotland's struggle for independence. The car park was built in 1995 during filming and the name has remained. It is an ideal starting point for several forest walks and cycling trails.

View from near The Braveheart Car Park

The walk to **The Wishing Stone** (see above) is a short, fairly level, walk from the car park and passes the **Old Nevis Graveyard.**

Dun Deardail is a longer walk. The path climbs steeply through the forest before emerging into a clearing on the summit where the remains of this Iron Age vitrified fort can be found. (A vitrified fort is one which has been fired to fuse the stones together.) The view down the glen from the top is well worth the climb. There are several duns of the same name scattered throughout the Highlands, some having an association with the legend of Deidre of The Sorrows.

All abilities trail

A short distance from the main car park is a **car park for the disabled**. From here a path leads directly to the **all abilities trail** – suitable for wheelchair users with assistance.

Cow Hill

This is the conical shaped hill between the town and Glen Nevis. A signposted trail from the Braveheart car park leads to the summit via "The Peat Path," so named because until recently it was the path used for access to the part of the hill where peats were cut for fuel. The TV relay transmitter for Fort William sits on the summit of the hill, from where there are panoramic views over the town and beyond.

Clan Cameron Burial Ground

There are many stories about the Camerons of Glen Nevis. Half a mile (800m) past the Wishing Stone, set back from the road on the right hand side, is a burial ground where many clan members were laid to rest.

The Glen Nevis Visitor Centre

Open all year round, the visitor centre provides a wealth of information with an excellent range of leaflets. The shop also sells maps, books, gifts etc. There are interesting and imaginative displays about

Glen Nevis Visitor Centre

the geology and history of the glen as well as wider Scottish history. One such is a tree trunk to represent the near hundred and fifty years between the 1745 uprising and the opening of the Forth Rail Bridge in 1890. The tree's natural rings are used as a circular time line. Visitor Centre staff are knowledgeable and can provide detailed advice and a local weather forecast for the Ben Nevis summit. Tel: 01397 705922. In the shop is an excellent book on the flowers of Ben Nevis, published by the John Muir Trust.

Outside is a large car park and pleasant picnic area. At one end a suspension bridge spans the river for access to the Ben Nevis track as well as less energetic river walks.

Glen Nevis Caravan and Camping Park

The park enjoys a spectacular location and has won several awards, including a prestigious David Bellamy conservation award. As well as camping and caravanning, there are self catering lodges and cottages and an on-site shop. A herd of shaggy Highland Cattle can often be found grazing next to the park.

Glen Nevis Restaurant & Lounge Bar

Glen Nevis Restaurant & Lounge Bar

Open daily between March and October (reduced opening in winter,) the restaurant has a varied menu whilst the lounge serves lighter meals and sandwiches daily from 12 noon. This is a comfortable place to eat and caters for most tastes. The bar has an excellent range of wines, draught beers and malt whiskies.

Café Beag

Café with a view!

Open daily from April until September, this is an excellent, fully licensed foodery in a stunning setting. All produce is locally sourced and everything is freshly prepared or baked on the premises. The speciality sandwiches, home-made soup and burgers made from local beef all take some beating!

Glen Nevis House

Used as a headquarters during the 1745 Jacobite rebellion, the original house was burned down by order of The Duke of Cumberland as a reprisal. Mrs. Cameron, the owner's wife, took as many valuables as possible and sought refuge in Samuel's Cave further up the glen. (See below.)

Dun Dige

Near Glen Nevis House, behind the restaurant, is a large, flat topped mound of earth and stones, about six feet high (2m) and surrounded by a shallow ditch known as a "saucer barrow." (OS grid ref: 126719) "Dun" is a fortified piece of high ground. This one is thought to be the remains of that of the MacSorlie chiefs, an early branch of Clan Cameron.

Forest Trails

As well as The West Highland Way which passes through The Nevis Forest on the southern side of the Glen, there are several other tracks and paths. It is a pleasant peaceful place where pine martens can sometimes be spotted. Within the forest (OS Grid ref: 124715) is a **Rocking Stone**, one of many such large pivot-mounted boulders to be found in Scotland. Their original purpose is not clear but they are thought to have connections with the Druids.

The Youth Hostel is very popular and booking is usually necessary. Although a two mile (3km) walk from Fort William, it does have the advantage of being one of the starting points of the Ben Nevis track. Approximately a mile (1.5km) past the youth hostel, on the far bank at a shallower part of the river, is an ancient **graveyard** of the Camerons. Several slate gravestones remain.

Almost a mile (1.5km) further on is a **picnic site** and further still the hamlet of **Achriabhach** is reached where there is a **car park.** It is well worth stopping here to walk over the bridge where the **Polldubh Waterfall,** also called The Lower Falls, cascades below the road. For the energetic (and properly shod and equipped) a path heads off from the car park for the steep climb up a picturesque glen into the **Mamores.**

The Lower Falls

The road continues across the bridge for a further mile and a quarter (2km) where it ends at **The Higher Falls Car Park.** Across the river can be seen a rocky crag which is the site of **Samuel's Cave** ("Uamh Shomhairle".) **"The Waterslide"** is also a prominent feature viewed from here – water running over 1160 feet (350m) down the surface of the granite.

The Head of the Glen

Nevis Gorge and Steall Waterfall

From the head of the glen a fairly easy path, which is signposted Kinlochleven, Corrour Station and Spean Bridge, continues into a dramatic narrow gorge which widens onto a level meadow. The path is relatively easy but there are steep

A warning sign!

drops and there have been accidents so care needs to be taken.

Across the river can be seen the hanging valley, **Coire a' Mhail,** from which the dramatic Steall waterfall drops into Glen Nevis. Also referred to as The Higher Falls of Nevis, its Gaelic name "An Steall Bàn" means "The White Spout." A single drop of over 390 feet (117m) makes this one of the highest waterfalls in Britain, the third highest in Scotland. The gorge and meadow are renowned for the variety of plants and wildlife which thrive here. Whilst golden eagles favour the higher reaches of the mountainside, the lower slopes provide ideal habitats for whinchats, ring ouzels, meadow pipits and some unusual butterflies. A hair raising three wire bridge, one wire for your feet and two to cling on to, crosses the River Nevis to a point just below the waterfall. (Yes, one of the cables did once snap!)

Whilst the majority of people return along the path, other intrepid and properly equipped souls continue through the gorge and beyond for the challenging walk to remote Corrour Station or to Kinlochleven or Spean Bridge.

The Ben Nevis Inn

The Ben Nevis Inn

By the side of the river at **Achintee,** the

Ben Nevis Inn is a ten minute walk via the pedestrian bridge from the visitor centre car park, or can be reached by road from Fort William. This is the main starting

Weather Forecasting stone !

point for the Ben Nevis track. The Inn is a cosy converted barn with a wood burning stove. The inn has bunk house accommodation and is a popular venue for live music. A wide variety of food is available between 12 noon and 9pm daily during the summer. Open Thursday – Sunday only during the winter months.

Toilets
Glen Nevis Visitor Centre

CLIMBING BEN NEVIS

Ben Nevis is 1342m (4406') high. The most popular ascent begins at Achintee Farm and follows the stony, five mile (8km) track constructed to service the meteorological observatory which was built on the summit in 1883. The track is known as "the tourist route" but this is still serious mountain walking and should not be undertaken lightly, ill

equipped or without the necessary navigational skills to follow the path in bad conditions. Fatalities have occurred when people have strayed off the path and fallen down gullies. While the weather below may be fairly benign, it is often very different four thousand feet up. It is advisable to seek advice from the Glen Nevis Visitor Centre, to take a suitable map and sensible clothing and to obtain the free safety leaflet. Serious climbers flock to the Ben's north face – at 1000 feet (300m) high and one and a quarter miles (2000m) wide it is Britain's largest cliff.

3.   NORTH EAST OF FORT WILLIAM

North west of the town the River Lochy and Telford's Caledonian Canal follow the cleft of the Great Glen, beyond which lie Glen Loy and picturesque Loch Arkaig: To the north east are The Nevis Range, Leanachan Forest and Glen Spean. The two sides of the canal offer very different routes and combining the two makes an extremely pleasant and interesting circular tour. The main A82 leaves Fort William for Spean Bridge and beyond, being the main route north. However, there are many interesting places along this route within a relatively short distance of Fort William.

The Great Glen, North of Fort William

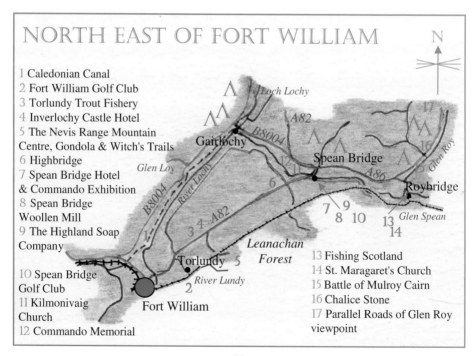

NORTH EAST OF FORT WILLIAM   N

1 Caledonian Canal
2 Fort William Golf Club
3 Torlundy Trout Fishery
4 Inverlochy Castle Hotel
5 The Nevis Range Mountain Centre, Gondola & Witch's Trails
6 Highbridge
7 Spean Bridge Hotel & Commando Exhibition
8 Spean Bridge Woollen Mill
9 The Highland Soap Company
10 Spean Bridge Golf Club
11 Kilmonivaig Church
12 Commando Memorial
13 Fishing Scotland
14 St. Maragaret's Church
15 Battle of Mulroy Cairn
16 Chalice Stone
17 Parallel Roads of Glen Roy viewpoint

Fort William Golf Club

Visitors are welcome at this 18 hole golf club. Situated at the base of Ben Nevis, don't be surprised if the scenery affects your concentration! Club and trolley hire available. Tel: 01397 704464.

Torlundy Trout Fishery

Two miles (3km) north of Fort William, this is a lovely tranquil place to try your hand at fly fishing. (It is also probably the best place for scenic water reflections of Ben Nevis!) Open for half day, full day or evening sessions, rod hire is available and tuition is reasonably priced. For anyone who has not tried fly fishing before, this is a wonderful way to begin in a truly glorious Highland farm setting.

Torlundy Trout Fishery

Inverlochy Castle Hotel is world renowned for luxurious comfort. For a memorable experience, lunch in the dramatic dining room or afternoon tea on the terrace is an experience not to be rushed. (Booking necessary except for the light lunch menu.) In a stunning location, overlooking its own private loch, the castle was originally built as a Scottish Baronial style home for the third Lord Abinger (William Frederick Scarlett.)

Construction of the castle began in 1863 and it remained in the family until the mid 1940's when it was sold to Joseph Hobbs who, at one time, owned the Ben Nevis distillery. The castle became a hotel in 1969.

Elegant surroundings: Inverlochy Castle

In addition to his distillery interest, in 1945 Hobbs was responsible for setting up the **Great Glen Cattle Ranch.** His idea was to create a Canadian style ranch of Aberdeen Angus bulls and Irish heifers. The remains of the two large cattle sheds which still bear the name "The Great Glen Cattle Ranch" can be seen by the side of the A82.

The River Lundy

A minor road leaves the A82 at Torlundy and heads east for a short distance before petering out into a track which follows the River Lundy for a further mile (1.5km) through the forest to the Nevis Range complex.

The Nevis Range

A cycle track and walking path links Fort William town centre with the Nevis Range four miles (6.5km) north east of Fort William. This is a huge outdoor activity complex centred on an eighty car **mountain gondola** system on the slopes of Aonach Mor which, along with Aonach

Beag, flanks Ben Nevis. It takes approximately fifteen minutes to travel the one and a half mile (2km), 2000 feet (650m) climb, with ever more spectacular views over the Great Glen and as far as The Inner Hebrides on a clear day. Originally favoured mainly by skiers, the complex now caters for a range of activities including snow-boarding, ice climbing, paragliding, hang gliding and mountain biking – the latter includes a hair-raising, World Cup trail down the mountain. For the less adventurous there are gentler bike trails (see below,) a mountain discovery centre, nature trails, way-marked mountain paths, a restaurant and bar and some spectacular views. For

Mountain gondola

The Nevis Range: Walks from the top

anyone who wishes to enjoy the mountain's dizzy heights the easy way, the Gondola ride is a great experience, with no obligation to do anything other than

enjoy the view. There is also a coffee shop and gift shop at the base station (as well as a bike wash!) Wheelchair users are able to access the gondolas and there are disabled toilets at both top and bottom stations. Opening times: (weather permitting) 10.00 am. - 5pm.daily. Closed for maintenance mid November to mid December. www.nevisrange.co.uk

Leanachan Forest

Owned by the forestry commission, Leanachan Forest is accessed by the road to the Nevis Range and is criss-crossed with walks and mountain bike trails. The **River Lundy** flows through the forest and one walk follows its path. The rare black and orange **Chequered Skipper butterfly** lives along its length, the damp river banks and birch and hazel trees providing an ideal habitat.

The Witch's Trails

The Witch's trails

The Witch of Leanachan is reputed to have taken up residence on the slopes of Aonach Mor during the 1800's. The trails are an exciting set of graded mountain biking trails through the forest at the foot of the Nevis Range. There is a separate Forestry Commission car park beyond the Nevis Range car park. Bike hire is available from either Witch's Trail Bike Hire or Alpine Bikes, both of whom have branches (summer only) on the approach road to the Nevis Range. The Forestry Commission have produced an excellent fold up trail guide which is available from the Nevis Range shop and from biking shops.

Mountain Biking Information

Run by Fort William's own World Champion mountain biker Alastair MacLennan, **MTB Ride Guide** offers skills courses or guided biking for all levels over the many trails around Fort William. For a chance to get right to the heart of the action, why not treat yourself and hire your own personal guide for a day or half day? www.mtbrideguide.com Another useful source of information is at www.ridefortwilliam.co.uk

Spean Bridge

Spean Bridge is a busy place where the A82 and A86 meet, the former continuing north up the Great Glen to Loch Ness and beyond whilst the A86 carries traffic eastwards for Aviemore, The Cairngorms and Speyside. The bridge referred to in the village name is one of Thomas Telford's bridges.

There is a well stocked convenience store, a post office, cash dispenser, a Little Chef café and a railway station, Spean Bridge being on the West Highland Railway line. The area has connections with the Jacobite uprising of 1745 and also more recent connections with the British Army Commandos: The surrounding hills and nearby Achnacarry formed the core of their training grounds during World War II. **"The Commando Trail"** is a leaflet which gives details about the locations

associated with them. There are several other places of interest in and around the village and it is easy to spend a full day or more here.

The Spean Bridge Hotel & Commando Exhibition

Commando Exhibition

The hotel has long since been associated with the Commandos, having been one of their "watering holes" during the war and present day troops still train in the area. Within the hotel is a small but fascinating exhibition dedicated to this elite band of men. As well as uniforms, an excellent collection of group photographs and a book of remembrance, there is also a collection of intriguing artefacts and "tools of the trade." These include original small arms training manuals and a morphine ampoule with the original instructions – the date and time of medication to be written on the casualty's forehead! The exhibition is open daily between 10am and 4.30pm.

In addition to the exhibition and **The Commando Bar and Bistro**, the hotel also has an outside takeaway cafe and an outdoor seating area.

Spean Bridge Woollen Mill

Tartan goods, Spean Bridge Woollen Mill

This is a large retail outlet for knitwear, Harris Tweed, clan tartan scarves, souvenirs and malt whiskies. An old loom is used on certain days for weaving demonstrations. As well as an indoor café, there is a nice seating area outside and, from the side of the building, good views of the picturesque arched road bridge over the River Spean.

The Highland Soap Company

The Highland Soap Compamy

(See also Fort William High Street section.)With retail outlets at Spean Bridge and Fort William, this is a "must visit" for beautiful organic soaps and other cosmetics.

Spean Bridge Golf Course

Although only nine holes, this course is known for being quite challenging, as well as for its glorious setting and spectacular mountain views. The course was designed

Spean bridge Golf Club

and built by locals during the 1950's. Visitors welcome.

The Old Station Restaurant

This is a nostalgic place to eat, the restaurant occupying the former station booking office and waiting room. Food is locally sourced, freshly cooked and an

The Old Station Restaurant

open fire adds to the olde worlde ambience, (as does the homemade bread and butter pudding.) Real ale enthusiasts will not be disappointed. Booking recommended.

Killiechonate Forest
Accessed from behind the railway station, Killiechonate is part of the larger Leanachan Forest. There are several footpaths and tracks and it is possible to follow one of the shorter woodland trails or to walk to Kinlochleven (18 miles/ 30km), Corrour Station (15 miles/24km) or Glen Nevis (18 miles/30km.)

There are also pleasant walks alongside the River Spean where bluebells and anemones thrive in the shade of the birch and conifer trees which line the river banks. A minor road follows the river, crossing the Coire an Eoin stream near to where it tumbles into the Spean amidst boulders and interesting rocks eroded by the water.

Interesting rock formations, River Spean

Russell's Restaurant is an award winning establishment with the emphasis on "modern Scottish." Particularly renowned for serving local game, lamb and fish, it is a pleasant change to find also an imaginative and varied vegetarian menu.

A place to savour the best of Scottish cuisine.

James McCallum Studio
Renowned Scottish artist James McCallum has his studio near Spean Bridge. Open by appointment. Tel: 01397 712690 (see also section on the Mallaig mural.)

Kilmonivaig Church

Kilmonivaig Church

Just north of the Spean Bridge on the A82, a lane to the left leads down to the picturesque Kilmonivaig Church, originally built in 1812 to replace an earlier one at Gairlochy. Kilmonivaig is the largest of the Scottish parishes although this is not reflected in the size of this pretty little white church, complete with bell housed in its own miniature belfry.

The Commando Memorial
Situated on the A82, a mile (1.5km) to the north west of Spean Bridge, this is an imposing sight – especially when floodlit at night. Set against a backdrop of Ben Nevis and the Grey Corries, the views from here are truly spectacular, including into The Great Glen. The seventeen feet (5m) high statue of three Commandos in

battledress was crafted in bronze by sculptor Scott Sutherland and unveiled in 1952 by Queen Elizabeth, The Queen Mother. It commemorates Commandos who trained in this area during World War II and on its plinth is carved the motto "UNITED WE CONQUER." A moving service is held here each year on Remembrance Sunday but the site is visited by many veterans and relatives throughout the year. In addition to the

main memorial is a small commemorative garden for individuals. From the memorial the B8004 runs to Gairlochy and beautiful Loch Arkaig. (See section on Caledonian Canal and Achnacarry.)

Commando Memorial

The Old Pines Hotel & Restaurant
Open to non-residents, (Feb – Oct.) a meal at the Old Pines is something special - whether for tea, coffee and scones or the full dinner menu. It is especially nice to find somewhere with such a varied and appealing light lunch menu, although the choice between sandwiches on homemade pumpkin seed bread, cheese and leek tart or a bowl of genuinely hand cut chips calls for some serious decision making! (Two hundred yards/175m along the B8004 towards Gairlochy road from the Commando Memorial.)

Highbridge
Two miles (3km) west of Spean Bridge, along the minor road to Kilmonivaig are the ruins of High Bridge over the Spean Gorge. The line of one of General Wade's military roads runs parallel to the A82. The bridge was built in 1736 by the general and replaced a ford at Insh which had previously been the river crossing for these parts. Wade's bridge was used until 1819 when the present bridge was constructed by Thomas Telford. Highbridge is famous as the place where the first shots of the 1745 uprising were fired. A nearby cairn records events of that day when Highlanders and a piper forced government troops to turn back. Although the middle of the bridge collapsed in 1913 it is still impressive.

Roybridge and Glen Roy
The River Roy joins the River Spean at Roybridge on the A86 which follows the original line of one of Telford's roads. Roybridge village has a general store, large Catholic church, two hotels and a particularly helpful post office. There are some lovely walks in and around Roybridge: There are paths on both sides of the River Spean but also by following the Bohenie road and then turning off onto the track into the **Achaderry Estate** there is a signed walk to a lochan where a wonderfully peaceful **picnic sit**e can be found. Roybridge railway station is the nearest one for exploring the dramatic **Monessie Gorge.**

The **Stronlossit Inn** serves excellent food, as well as teas and coffees. Equally welcoming is the **Roybridge Hotel** which serves traditional "pub grub" in the Roy Bar between 6pm and 9pm. (Open all year.)

The Grey Corries Lodge is a bunkhouse

with budget accommodation, wood burning stove, drying room, kitchen etc.

Fishing Scotland

A truly memorable "Highland experience," this is the chance for beginners to hire their own private tutor or, for experienced anglers to fish some of the best fly fishing rivers in the country with their own personal guide. Reservations essential. www.fishing-scotland.co.uk Tel: 01397 712812

St. Margaret's Church and Chapel House. Just off the main road stands an imposing early twentieth century Catholic church and adjoining chapel house. It was designed by Reginald Fairlie and built in 1929. Margaret was the eleventh century Queen of Malcolm III. She was a pious woman and carried out much charitable work but was also instrumental in converting her husband and introducing reforms to the Scottish Church. Although dedicated to St. Margaret, the church here also has direct connections with another saint, recently canonised. Within the grounds of the church is a shrine to **Blessed Mary MacKillop**, whose father left Roybridge for Australia. Mary was born there and became a nun, working with the needy children and prostitutes. She founded The Order of The Sisters of St. Joseph and was beatified (the first step towards becoming a saint) in 1995. In October 2010 she was canonised in Rome to become Australia's first saint.

The Glenspean Lodge Hotel was once a favourite hunting lodge of one of Scotland's largest estates. King Edward V11 visited here as a guest of Laird Mackintosh, whose portrait still hangs here. Today it is a modern, comfortable hotel set in five acres of gardens and with a sauna, Jacuzzi and snooker room.

Glen Roy

Glen Roy

Glen Spean and Glen Roy are both of particular historical and geological interest. From Roybridge a narrow road heads up Glen Roy. Possibly not for faint hearted drivers, the scenery is some of the best in Scotland and gives one a real sense of being a part of the grandeur rather than a mere onlooker. It was down Glen Roy that Montrose and his followers came in 1645 to surprise Argyll at Inverlochy. It was also in Glen Roy that the last inter-clan battle was fought in 1688, **The Battle of Mulroy,** when the MacDonells defeated the Mackintoshes. A **roadside**

St. Margaret's Church

cairn commemorates the event.

Roadside Cairn: The Battle of Mulroy

Another interesting feature just off the road on the right hand side (GR 295847) is the **Glen Roy Chalice Stone,** a roughly rectangular rock with a chalice engraved on one side. Such rocks were used as secret altars by Catholic priests when Catholics were being persecuted and had to worship in secret.

The road climbs steeply, past some old croft buildings to a viewpoint facing the famous **"Parallel Roads of Glen Roy"** – a series of strange lines (actually scree strewn ledges) along the side of the glen. They run exactly parallel to each other, the top two about eighty feet (25m) apart, the bottom one some two hundred feet (60m) lower. Originally thought to have been etched into the mountain side by giants, the lines actually mark three different levels of ancient shores formed when the valleys here were filled by massive lochs held back by glacial dams. Excellent interpretive boards at the viewpoint explain and illustrate the extent of the glaciation and how the unusual landmarks were formed. The road continues to remote Brunachan, once the site of a quarry which produced querns – the large flat stones used in corn mills.

NB: To complete a circular tour, incorporating the section on "The Caledonian Canal and Achnacarry," take the B8004 from the **Commando Memorial**.

Old croft cottage in Glen Roy

The Parallel Roads of Glen Roy

Public Toilets
Behind Spean Bridge Mill (customers)
The Nevis Range – top and bottom of Gondola ride

4. THE CALEDONIAN CANAL AND ACHNACARRY

The Caledonian Canal is a spectacular example of nineteenth century engineering. Linking the Atlantic Ocean with the North Sea, it is arguably the crowning glory of Thomas Telford's achievements. As well as providing a safe alternative to braving the stormy seas around the top of Scotland, the building of the canal was planned to provide employment at a time when many Highlanders were almost destitute. It was begun in 1803, before the existence of huge earth moving machines so was dug out by men with nothing more mechanised than picks and shovels. Not just one canal, it is a series of artificial waterways linking the lochs of the Great Glen to make one continuous route from Corpach, near Fort William, to the Beauly Firth on the east coast at Inverness. The project involved the construction of twenty-nine locks, ten bridges and four aqueducts. It was navigable from 1822, having cost three times the amount estimated. Since 1962 the canal has been owned by British Waterways who have repaired and refurbished it. It is now busier than ever, mostly with pleasure craft and its towpath is a favourite route for walkers and cyclists.

The Caledonian Canal

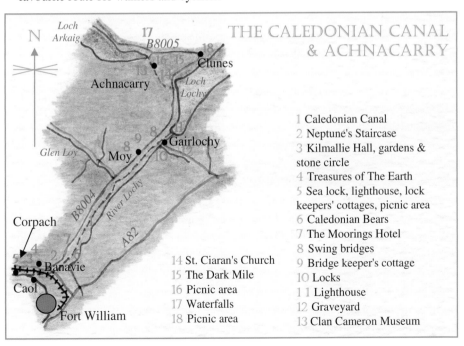

THE CALEDONIAN CANAL & ACHNACARRY

1 Caledonian Canal
2 Neptune's Staircase
3 Kilmallie Hall, gardens & stone circle
4 Treasures of The Earth
5 Sea lock, lighthouse, lock keepers' cottages, picnic area
6 Caledonian Bears
7 The Moorings Hotel
8 Swing bridges
9 Bridge keeper's cottage
10 Locks
11 Lighthouse
12 Graveyard
13 Clan Cameron Museum
14 St. Ciaran's Church
15 The Dark Mile
16 Picnic area
17 Waterfalls
18 Picnic area

Corpach

Two miles (3km) along the Mallaig road, Corpach has much to recommend it, not just as somewhere to pass through on the way to Skye and beyond. Corpach is at the head of both Loch Linnhe and Loch Eil, situated where the two meet. It is also the southern end of the Caledonian Canal where ships pass through the sea lock from Loch Linnhe into the first section of artificial waterway to Loch Lochy.

The sea lock was completed in 1819 with the original lock gates built of Welsh oak. By 1906 these had been replaced by gates reinforced with steel. At the entrance to the canal is a small lighthouse and whitewashed lock keepers' houses designed by Telford. The lock is now mechanised. On the seaward bank, accessed across one of the locks, is a pleasant **picnic area** with views back to Fort William and Ben Nevis.

The Sea Lock, Corpach

The name "Corpach" means "The Place of Bodies." This could refer to an early tradition in this part of Scotland when burials took place on islands. "Important" people were taken to Iona and Corpach was one of the places from which they began this final journey, having been carried many miles from the north and east. Corpach is part of the parish of Kilmallie, one of Scotland's largest.

During World War II there was a large naval base at Corpach, HMS St. Christopher. In 1965 the site became a wood pulping mill providing employment for nearly a thousand people until it closed in 1980. Today the village is a popular place to stay with a variety of accommodation including B and B's and two hostels/bunkhouses.

Looking towards Ben Nevis

Rockhopper Sea Kayaking

This company provides unforgettable adventures for experienced kayakers as well as instruction for novices. Overnight expeditions are also popular. Large, double kayaks are available for young children or nervous adults.

Kilmallie Hall

Like many community centres in this part of the world, Kilmallie Hall also serves as a **visitor centre**. There is a large car park (turn off the main road at the boat full of plants) where there are some excellent **information boards** about the Great Glen and the Road to The Isles. Within the hall are public toilets, and a **café** which opens several mornings a week for tea, coffee, soup and home baking.

Kilmallie Hall Gardens

The hall is set amidst attractive gardens which have been developed by the community. They include a memorial garden, a **maze,** a woodland walk, **picnic tables** and a modern **stone circle** representing the geology of the Highlands and Islands. Included in the circle are boulders as diverse as gabro from Mull, slate from Ballachulish, Skye marble and serpentinite from Drumnadrochit. The circle is designated as part of a European and Global **Geopark.**

A modern stone circle

A cairn to mark Queen Elizabeth's Golden Jubilee in June 2002 was constructed by children of the parish. The gardens are wheelchair friendly.

Treasures of The Earth

Treasures of The Earth, Corpach

This is a dazzling exhibition of precious and semi precious gemstones, housed in various imaginative settings including simulated caves and mines. As well as being visually impressive, it is very informative.

The Snowgoose Mountain Centre runs residential and day courses for families, groups or individuals in kayaking, walking and climbing, as well as expeditions on land and water and wilderness expeditions in the hills.

The railway crossing at Corpach is a good place from which to watch the **Jacobite Steam Train** going past in summer.

The "Jacobite" at Corpach

Caol

Situated on the side of Loch Linnhe, Caol is a real find. There are fabulous views towards Fort William and Ben Nevis and a selection of useful shops and facilities away from the town centre and consequently far less crowded. As well as a post office, pharmacy, launderette and convenience store, there is a flower shop and a choice of places to eat including Chinese, Indian and the award winning Sammy's Fish 'N' Chip Shop. For anyone who enjoys being creative, "Togs" is a must – an Aladdin's cave of craft and haberdashery items. Caol has a beach and a pleasant walk is to go along this to Corpach and return via the canal towpath.

Banavie & Neptune's Staircase

Banavie, one meaning being "white or clear water," is an exciting place: Staircase

Neptune's Staircase

locks are those which consist of a run of locks, the top gate of each forming the bottom gate of the next. The Caledonian Canal has three such sets and **Neptune's Staircase** is the most impressive. A swing bridge carries the road over the Caledonian Canal at the bottom of the locks and then eight locks raise the vessels a total of over seventy feet (21m) in less than half a mile (800m.) The large car park nearby makes a good base from which to enjoy a walk along the

Mobile information!

canal in either direction. Caledonian Canal tourist information is available as a mobile phone application – see the notice board on the car park near the entrance to the towpath.

At one time several passenger steamers passed daily through the locks on their way between Glasgow and Inverness. Today it is mainly pleasure craft that negotiate the locks, an interesting spectacle for onlookers. **Banavie Railway Station** is at the foot of the locks but in 1901, when the Mallaig line opened, the line ran to the top of the locks to connect with the steam ferries berthing there.

The Lochy Bar & Restaurant

Two hundred yards (180m) from Neptune's Staircase, on Kilmallie Road, is the Lochy Bar & Restaurant - a popular, child and dog friendly place with a reasonably priced menu for eating inside, at the picnic area or to take away. The **beer garden** enjoys good views of Ben Nevis.

Caledonian Bears

Caledonian Bears

Along the towpath beside Neptune's Staircase is "The Old Smiddy," one of Telford's canal-side buildings. It is now home to Caledonian Bears – a unique and delightful collection of handmade Scottish teddies dressed in tweeds and tartans reminiscent of rural Scotland in days gone by. Teas and coffees are available here and a dog-friendly water bowl outside

Telford's "Smiddy" building

welcomes canine teddy lovers!

The Moorings Hotel
The Moorings Hotel offers a choice of dining options including the award winning **Neptune's Restaurant.** Bar meals are served all day in the **Upper Deck Lounge Bar** or in a canal-side garden for alfresco dining. The Moorings has a reputation for being consistently good, having achieved an AA Rosette for many consecutive years.
The B8004 leaves Banavie to run parallel

The Caledonian Canal

to the Caledonian Canal and River Lochy. To the south east are wonderful views of Ben Nevis and ahead is something of interest and an even more picturesque view with every twist in the road. For engineering enthusiasts there are several interesting features along this stretch of the canal: Approximately one and a half miles (2km) north east of Banavie is an **aquaduct** which carries the canal over the Sheangain Burn. Midway between Banavie and Gairlochy, **Glen Loy** runs off to the north west with **forest trails** and tracks where pine martens can often be seen. The River Loy passes underneath the canal at Strone to join the River Lochy. At Moy is a **cast iron swing bridge** which was built in pieces and assembled here in 1821. It consists of two separate halves and a bridge keeper is employed solely to operate the bridge: This involves opening one half and then rowing to the other side of the canal to open the other half! The nearby **bridge keeper's cottage** has windows in both ends to give views up and down the canal.

Gairlochy
There is a further **swing bridge** at Gairlochy between the two locks, the final one opening on to **Loch Lochy.** An interesting **information board** tells of the history of this particular section of the canal. At the very end of this stretch is a small **lighthouse.** It is a short but pleasant walk along the towpath for a superb view up the length of Loch Lochy. Down the hill a short way from the swing bridge is an interesting old **graveyard** but with no signs of there having been a building there.
During the first Jacobite rebellion of 1689

Gairlochy Swing Bridge

Viscount Dundee gathered the Highland Clans near Gairlochy before himself being killed in battle, in spite of having led the clans to a resounding victory.

Gairlochy Bottom Lock

Loch Lochy

The B8004 crosses the bridge at Gairlochy towards Spean Bridge while the B8005 continues along the western shore of Loch Lochy, lined with silver birch trees. One of the lesser visited lochs, it is the third deepest loch in Scotland, one of the most picturesque and reputedly home to Lizzie – sister of Nessie, the Loch Ness monster!

Achnacarry

Achnacarry is the true heart of Cameron country. The Camerons were staunch supporters of the Jacobite cause and in 1745 over one thousand men marched from Achnacarry and Loch Arkaig to Glenfinnan to join Bonnie Prince Charlie. **Achnacarry Castle**, nestling in the trees, is the home of the Chief of Clan Cameron, also known as Lochiel. The house was designed by Scottish architect Gillespie Graham. While many of the great Highland families lost their lands over the centuries, Clan Cameron did not. From 1942 this was where soldiers of the **Commando units** underwent rigorous training in the uncompromising terrain of the area. Winston Churchill instigated the creation of this elite force to undertake special missions behind enemy lines. The Clan Chief, Sir Donald Cameron of Lochiel, and his family moved out of the castle to another residence nearby. Over twenty-five thousand men of various nationalities were trained here, the bleak countryside being the perfect place to learn survival skills. After the war the Camerons returned to their home. Achnacarry Castle is not open to the public but a short distance away is the Clan Cameron Museum

The Clan Cameron Museum

The Clan Cameron Museum

Housed in a white painted croft cottage dating from the seventeenth century and which served as the post office during WWII, this is a truly delightful museum. There is a fine collection of artefacts

Bonnie Prince Charlie

connected with Clan Cameron and The Queen's Own Cameron Highlanders, as well as with the Commandos. One exhibit is a pair of boots in remarkably good condition as the footwear had belonged to Sir Ewen Dubh who died in 1719! The museum has a section devoted to Prince Charles Edward Stuart, including a life sized reproduction of one of his hiding places, a red waistcoat actually worn by him and a ring with a secret compartment which opens to reveal a portrait of the Prince. The small museum shop is stocked with an excellent range of tasteful gifts and souvenirs. Open April – Mid Oct.

The Commando Trail

Although the grounds of Achnacarry Castle are private, an interesting trail takes visitors to some of the main training areas. Leaflets are available at the museum.

St. Ciaran's Church

Also called St. Kiaran's, Achnacarry's lovely church is one of several in Scotland dedicated to the sixth century Irish saint who was a carpenter by trade and a protégé of

St. Columba. Achnacarry is part of the Kilmallie Parish. The church was designed by Peter Macgregor Chalmers

St. Ciaran's Church, interior

and built in 1911. It is set in woodland a short distance from the museum, a handmade sign directing the way. The

St. Ciaran's Church

entrance is through the tower at one end and there is a small room above the entrance for the minister. The interior is simple but there are three stained glass windows. Although a service is usually held only once a month, the church is lovingly cared for with usually more than one display of fresh flowers.

Clunes

Where the B8005 turns west away from Loch Lochy is the small settlement of Clunes and a Forestry Commission car

47

park with **forest trails**, one of which follows the wooded shoreline of **Loch Lochy.**

Loch Lochy near Clunes

The Dark Mile

The road westwards between Clunes and Loch Arkaig (B8005) is known as the Dark Mile (Mile Dorche.) It is an atmospheric road along the heavily wooded and steeply sided glen between Lochs Arkaig and Lochy. It owes its name to the fact that it is so heavily wooded that direct sunlight rarely penetrates. The stone walls along the roadside are thickly covered in moss, adding to the gloomy atmosphere. The conifers which line the road replaced earlier beech trees. The road has associations with Bonnie Prince Charlie: After the Battle of Culloden in 1746 the prince sought refuge with the Camerons at Clunes and is said to have hidden in a cave in the hills to the north.

Eas Chia-Aig Falls

Where the road meets Loch Arkaig there is another forestry commission car park with **information boards** about the woodlands. Clunes Forest here is being restored to original Scots Pine and is a favourite place for red squirrels who thrive on pine nuts, removing the scales from pine cones with their sharp teeth to reveal the seeds inside. There is a **picnic area** and a path leading from the car park to the top of the **Eas Chia-aig Falls** (also called Cia-Aig.) Below the falls is a deep pool known as **The Witch's Cauldron.** Legend tells of a witch who was chased over the falls and into the pool by Cameron farmers after she had placed a curse on their cattle. The same waterfalls feature in the film "Rob Roy."

Loch Arkaig

Loch Arkaig has a feeling of being very remote, especially if one travels the narrow thirteen mile (21km) road to its western end. However, it is easily accessed by the B8004 Gairlochy road from the Commando Memorial or from the other end of the B8004 which leaves Banavie. Gold to fund Jacobite endeavours was reputedly hidden in Loch Arkaig (but never found.) Many Commando training exercises took place on the loch. Along the northern shore is a **butterfly conservation area** with a marked trail and the chance to spot some rare species.

NB: To complete a circular tour incorporating the section on "North of Fort William" return to Gairlochy and take the B8004 to Spean Bridge, via the **Commando Memorial.**

Toilets
Killmallie Parish hall
Caol Shopping Centre
Clan Cameron Museum
Wifi hot spots
Banavie Locks

5.   THE ROAD TO THE ISLES

"The Road To The Isles" is the name given to the A830 between Fort William and Mallaig. Banavie and Corpach have already been included in the section on the canal so we now join the Road To The Isles just west of Corpach.

Until the eighteenth century Scotland had few proper roads. Between 1724 and 1740 General Wade, under orders from King George I, oversaw the construction of many Scottish "military" roads but it was not until the early nineteenth century that there was anything resembling today's road system. In 1803 the newly created Commission for Highland Roads and Bridges appointed Thomas Telford as their engineer. New "parliamentary roads" were to be funded jointly by land owners and the government. One such was the road westwards from Fort William. When completed in 1812, it ended at Arisaig. Only with the arrival of the railway in 1901 did the road continue to Mallaig. The route passes through part of "The Rough Bounds" ("Na Garbh Chriochan,") the isolated area between Loch Hourn and Loch Shiel and an area steeped in romance and history: It was here that Charles Edward Stuart landed and mustered support before the ill-fated Battle of Culloden. It was also where he made his subsequent flight before leaving for France, never to return.

Followed closely by the line of the railway, the route is one of the most picturesque in the country. It is a triumph of engineering, with dramatic bridges and viaducts alternating with sections hewn through solid rock. The construction of the railway involved blasting no less than eleven tunnels. Until recently, the road was fairly hazardous: It was narrow, with many tight bends and much of it single track. In recent years it has been greatly improved.

Whatever the time of year, the scenery is breathtaking with an ever changing array of colours: In May and June the verges are vibrant blue with bluebells. As these fade, bright yellow gorse appears: Next come the brilliant reds of the mountain ash berries, in turn succeeded by the muted mauves and tans of heather and bracken as summer draws to a close. The route skirts lochs large and small and passes beneath towering mountains before dropping down to Arisaig. There it meets the west coast with its rock skerries, white beaches, sparkling seas and views out to the islands of Eigg, Rum, Muck and Skye. The road and railway end at Mallaig, a lively fishing port and gateway to Skye and the Outer Hebrides.

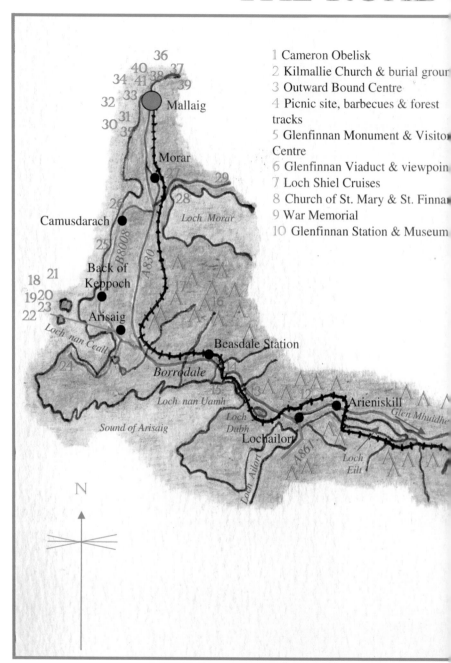

36
40 38 37
34 41 39
32 33
30 31 Mallaig
35

Morar
27 29

26 28
Camusdarach Loch Morar

25
Back of
Keppoch B8008
A830

18 21
19 20 17 16
22 23
Arisaig

Beasdale Station

24 14
Borrodale
15 13 12 Arieniskill
Loch nan Uamh Glen Mhuidhe
Sound of Arisaig Loch
Dubh
Lochailort A861 Loch
Loch Ailort Eilt

1 Cameron Obelisk
2 Kilmallie Church & burial groun
3 Outward Bound Centre
4 Picnic site, barbecues & forest
tracks
5 Glenfinnan Monument & Visitor
Centre
6 Glenfinnan Viaduct & viewpoin
7 Loch Shiel Cruises
8 Church of St. Mary & St. Finnar
9 War Memorial
10 Glenfinnan Station & Museum

N

11 Station Dining Car
12 Susan McCallum Memorial
13 Our Lady of The Braes
14 Loch nan Uamh Viaduct
15 The Prince's Cairn
16 Sgurr an Albanaich
17 Sgurr an t Sasunnaich
18 Land, Sea & Island Centre
19 SOE Memorial
20 Arisaig Marine
21 Small Isles ferry
22 St. Mary's Catholic Church
23 St. Maelrubha's Chapel
24 The Rhu of Arisaig
25 Traigh Golf Course

26 Silver Sands of Morar
27 The Morar Cross
28 Fishing/boat hire
29 Loch Morar Crafts
30 Mallaig Visitor Centre
31 Mallaig Heritage Centre
32 Jaffy's Kippers
33 St. Columba's Church
34 Swimming pool
35 RNLI Gift Shop
36 Railway station
37 Mallaig Harbour Mural
38 Fisherman & Child sculpture
39 MV The Grimsay Isle
40 Bruce Watt Sea Cruises
41 Caledonian MacBrayne Ferry Terminal

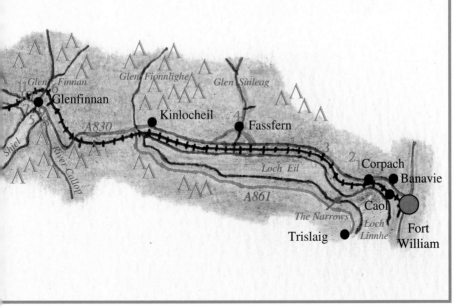

Cameron Obelisk, Kilmallie

The Cameron Obelisk

Just west of Corpach, clearly visible from the road, is a large obelisk dedicated to Colonel John Cameron of Fassfern who was killed at the Battle of Quatre Bras in 1815, just before Waterloo. Beneath the monument is a transcription of the words of the original plaque which, although chiselled in stone, have now worn away. The Colonel's "mortal remains" were transported here "from the field of glory where he died." A lengthy citation details his great bravery leading the 92nd Regiment of Scottish Highlanders. The final words are thought to have been written by Sir Walter Scott: *"Reader, call not his fate untimely, who, thus honoured and lamented, closed a Life of Fame by a Death of Glory."*

Kilmallie Church

Just above the obelisk is Kilmallie Parish Church, probably dating from 1783 although there have been several churches on this site, since 1296. Across the lane, over a small burn, is a burial ground where the remains of one former chapel, now covered in ivy are thought to date from the sixteenth century. The elaborate tomb of John Telford is found here - an engineer who worked on the Caledonian Canal and

Kilmallie Burial Ground

a relative of **Thomas Telford**. Another grave is that of nineteenth century poet **Mary Cameron MacKellar** who was born on the shores of Loch Eil and whose most notable work was a book of Gaelic poems and songs published in 1881.

Loch Eil

Beyond Corpach are **The Narrows** – where Loch Linnhe and Loch Eil meet at right angles. Loch Eil is a peaceful loch between gently sloping hills. The road is lined with birch trees and stately oaks. On the loch are usually several fish farms: The temperature of the water here is particularly suited to the cultivation of mussels. Road and railway run parallel to the shore past the **Outward Bound Centre**, an outdoor training school occupying the impressive house and grounds of Achdalieu Lodge, a shooting lodge built in 1885 by Cameron of Lochiel. An infamous skirmish is said to have occurred here in 1654 when soldiers from the garrison at Fort William arrived and began to cut down trees which belonged to Sir Ewen Cameron. The officer in charge and Sir Ewen ended up locked in combat. Just when it looked as though the clan chief would be beaten he managed to sink his teeth into the officer's throat and came away with a mouthful of flesh!

Fassfern

A small road, signposted to Fassfern, forms a loop which rejoins the A830 a mile (800m) further on. Fassfern makes a pleasant detour, especially if equipped for a barbecue as the picnic site here has built-in **barbecues**. There are forest tracks to explore and a seven mile (11km) right of way through the forest to **Glen Loy**. In spring the whole area is a riot of delicate Mayflowers.

Fassfern is another place where Bonnie Prince Charlie spent a night and here he is reputed to have picked a white wild rose, which became the emblem of the '45 uprising, known as the "white cockade." (A cockade is a rosette or knot of ribbons worn in a hat.)

Stone from a quarry on the Fassfern Estate was used for some of the buildings along the Caledonian Canal.

Barbecue picnic site at Fassfern

Kinlocheil, at the head of Loch Eil, is where Charles Edward Stuart stayed with his supporters a week after raising his father's standard at Glenfinnan. The imposing **Beinn an t-Sneachda** rises steeply from the roadside and the road crosses the River Fionn Lighe which runs into the loch. From near the bridge a track runs north to follow the river up **Glen Fionn Lighe**. To the south, the A861 branches off round the far side of the loch towards Strontian and Corran past **Trislaig,** from where a small ferry crosses Loch Linnhe to Fort William.

Beyond Loch Eil, the road continues westwards and towards ever more dramatic landscapes. To the south are the towering peaks of Meall nan Maigheach, Glas Bheinn and Meall nan Damh. This is red deer country, especially in the winter months when the herds leave the mountains for the lower slopes and can be quite a hazard for drivers.

One and a half miles (2km) before Glenfinnan, (near where the road passes beneath the railway) is a **picnic site** from which a footpath leads south to follow the **Callop River** through the **Loch Shiel Pinewoods**, home to otters and also a good place to see dragonflies and even pine martens. Non native conifers are gradually being felled to be replaced by native pines. For a longer walk, this path eventually joins a track which follows the **Cona Glen** all the way back to Loch Linnhe.

Glenfinnan (Glean Fhioghain)

Glenfinnan stands at the head of Loch Shiel, just under twenty miles (32km) from Fort William and where three glens meet. Loch Shiel is a long, freshwater loch which stretches almost to the sea and which forms the boundary between Argyll and Inverness-shire. Glenfinnan has several claims to fame but its greatest is its association with Charles Edward Stuart, Bonnie Prince Charlie. There is a lot to see and do in Glenfinnan so do allow time to enjoy it.

The Glenfinnan Monument is a tall, slender tower, atop which stands a statue of a highlander in a kilt. The monument commands an imposing view down the length of Loch Shiel and commemorates the spot where, on August 19th 1745, Prince Charles Edward Stuart met his Highland supporters, raised his father's red and white silk standard and declared him James III of England. Thus began the ill fated Jacobite campaign to reclaim the throne of England. (See inset section on Bonnie Prince Charlie.) The monument

The Glenfinnan Monument

was built in 1815, by Alexander MacDonald of Glenaladale in memory of all the men who had fought for the Jacobite cause. Many of the stones for the monument came from cairns at Glenfinnan built by men as they marched off. Each man placed a stone as he left and removed one on his return: What was left in each case was a cairn built by the men who had given their lives for the cause. The monument is now in the keeping of the National Trust for Scotland. There is a charge for climbing the tower - tickets are available from the visitor centre.

Glenfinnan Visitor Centre
The National Trust Visitor Centre (Open April - October) is across the road from the monument. There is a car park, gift shop, exhibitions about the Jacobite Campaign, toilets and a café. From the car park there are several walks which are detailed on information boards. Behind the centre the famous Glenfinnan Viaduct curves across the glen.

Loch Shiel Walk/Cycle
From near the monument are signposted walks to **Callop** one and half miles (2.5km) and **Polloch** twelve and a half miles (20km.) The latter is a beautiful route along the shore of the loch and through the forest. It is possible to arrange to be picked up by Loch Shiel Cruises for the return journey. Tel: 01687 470322 Mobile 07801 537617

Glenfinnan Viaduct
The iconic Glenfinnan Viaduct is one of Scotland's most photographed scenes. It is four hundred and sixteen yards (374m) long and has twenty-one arches, the highest of which is a hundred and ten feet (33m) above the river. It was completed in 1901 and curves elegantly across the glen, carrying the railway over the River Finnan. It continually surprises people to learn that the viaduct is built not of stone but of concrete, made by mixing cement with the material dug out from railway cuttings. It was designed by rail and road

Glenfinnan Viaduct

engineer Robert McAlpine who became known as "Concrete Bob." The viaduct has starred in several films: The opening shots for the 2001 film Charlotte Gray showed the viaduct and the loch. Set during the WWII, it is about a young Scottish woman who joined The French Resistance to rescue her RAF boyfriend. Perhaps even better known are the Harry Potter films, two of which include scenes shot here – Harry Potter and the Chamber of Secrets and Harry Potter and the Prisoner of Azkaban.
Scenes from the 1948 film Bonnie Prince Charlie were also shot in the area, very close to where the actual events occurred in 1745 but not, of course, featuring the viaduct.

Glenfinnan Viaduct Viewpoint

A path leads from the National Trust Centre to a viewpoint near the viaduct. The steep climb is worth it for the views of the monument and the loch, although perhaps the best view of all is from the train as it crosses the viaduct and often obligingly stops while people take photographs!

The Glenfinnan Estate

Deer management notice

At the bottom of the hill, opposite the entrance to the Glenfinnan House Hotel, is a small car park on the edge of the Glenfinnan Estate. Walkers and cyclists are welcomed to the estate and there are signposted tracks. The estate is part of the West Lochaber Deer Management Group and an information board gives details. It is possible to follow the estate road to Corryhully and then on to Loch Arkaig. It is also the access point for ascending Beinn an Tuim.

Glenfinnan House Hotel

Glenfinnan House Hotel

Formerly an eighteenth century mansion house, the hotel retains its full character and has grounds stretching down to the shores of Loch Shiel. There are stunning views towards the Glenfinnan Monument at the head of the loch and, in the other direction, down the length of the loch – views enjoyed from both the award winning restaurant and the lounge bar. The hotel is owned by the MacFarlane family, Gaelic speaking musicians who regularly hold musical evenings. Tel: 01397 722235. Access to Loch Shiel and the cruises is down the lane beyond the hotel.

Loch Shiel Cruises

A boat trip on Loch Shiel is the ultimate way to see this area, much of which is inaccessible other than by walking or by boat. Sailing right into the heart of Moidart, the scenery is breathtaking, the loch stretching between mountains which in places rise almost sheer from the water. Between April and October the MV Sileas plies up and down the loch. A knowledgeable skipper makes this a

Loch Shiel Cruises

church was built by another MacDonald of Glenaladale and consecrated in 1873. Inside are memorial stones to both the MacDonalds and to the Prince, the former having sheltered the latter. The church bell, which is mounted on a wooden frame in the grounds, was cast in 1878 by the Eagle Foundry of Dublin and bears the image of an Irish wolfhound.

memorable trip with a good chance of spotting red deer, golden eagles, the rare black-throated diver and other wildlife. Covered and open seating, an onboard toilet and a bar serving drinks and light refreshments make for a comfortable trip. Tel: 01687 470322 Mob: 07801 537617

Glenfinnan Church

Glenfinnan War Memorial
Near the church is a war memorial which, like many others in the area, has on top a statue of a soldier in a kilt. He is standing, head bowed, with "reversed arms" – his rifle held in reverse to signify mourning.

Glenfinnan War Memorial

Glenfinnan RC Church

The Catholic Church of St. Mary and St. Finnan is part of the Roman Catholic Diocese of Argyll and The Isles and stands high above Loch Shiel. It is a beautiful Gothic building designed by Edward Welby Pugin whose father designed The House of Commons. The

Glenfinnan Station
The entire station, its buildings now "listed," has been lovingly restored to its original state by John Barnes, who fell in love with the line as a teenager. The pretty chalet style buildings and platforms are exactly as they were, right down to contemporary suitcases stacked on the platform. In summer, the daily arrival of the Jacobite steam train completes the picture. The old booking office now

The Station Museum

houses the fascinating **Station Museum** which tells the story of The West Highland Line, including the construction of Glenfinnan Viaduct. There is also an interesting souvenir and book shop. Two immaculately refurbished carriages house the station dining car and a sleeping car available for holiday accommodation, as it has been since the 1950's. The museum is open daily June – mid October 9.00 – 17.00 or by appointment. A signposted woodland walk from nearby leads to a viewpoint.

The Station Dining Car
For freshly prepared food, home baking, and a nostalgic setting this is a hard one to beat. From a hearty "Rolling Stock" breakfast to a warming dish of "Station Master's Broth" or a "Tracklayer's Lunch," all appetites and tastes are well catered for. The fresh flowers are an additional nice touch. Open daily from May – October. (Watch out also for the evening specials.)

The Station Dining Car

The Prince's House Hotel
Once a seventeenth century staging house where coaches were provided with fresh horses, the hotel is mentioned in Dane Love's book "The Auld Inns of Scotland."

There are some interesting old photographs in the lounge as well as a large mural of a deer. It is a friendly, family owned hotel offering accommodation as well as dinners and light lunches cooked by the chef/proprietor. The emphasis is on good food, simply cooked to enhance rather than disguise quality local produce. Open Easter – mid September. Booking necessary. Tel: 01397 722246

The road climbs out of Glenfinnan before dropping down into **Glen Mhuidhe** (a good place for train spotters) and then on to Loch Eilt.

Glen Mhuidhe

Loch Eilt
Loch Eilt ("The Hind's Loch") must surely be one of Scotland's prettiest lochs. Framed by gigantic jagged peaks, the loch is dotted with tiny islets covered in pine trees. The road and railway separate, the latter following the southern shore while the road clings to the opposite one. This stretch of road is particularly dramatic in wet weather - streams and waterfalls tumble down steep craggy outcrops and rush under the road to join Loch Eilt which was once renowned as one of Europe's best lochs for sea trout fishing.

Nowadays its fish population consists mainly of brown trout. (Fishing permits

Loch Eilt

necessary.) Bonnie Prince Charlie is said to have sheltered under an ancient oak tree near the road.

An interesting collection of roadside cairns (OS GR802827) include one to mark the spot where friends and servants of Duncam Cameron of Inverailort, on the day of his funeral in 1874, carried his body to the edge of his property on the north side of the loch. From this point it was conveyed by hearse to the burial ground at Kilmallie.

Roadside Cairns

At the western end of Loch Eilt, at **Arieniskill,** the railway rejoins the road.

A track runs north into the wild country between Lochs Eilt and Morar. Another cave where Prince Charles took refuge is marked on the map at GR795850. It is thought that he spent three days here after fleeing from Culloden. A three mile (5km) long path runs above the western end of **Loch Beoraid** before dropping down to follow the **River Meoble** past Meoble Lodge and onto **Loch Morar.** The lodge was used during WWII as a training school for the SOE (Special Operations Executive.) French agents trained here in sabotage methods. This is wild country and only properly equipped, experienced walkers should attempt it. Unless returning the same way it would be necessary to arrange to be picked up by boat from the pier at Camus Luinge.

Loch Ailort

Loch Ailort is a sea loch which opens into The Sound of Arisaig. At the head of the loch the A861 leads off to the **Moidart Peninsula** and remote **Ardnamurchan Point,** the most westerly point on mainland Britain. From the head of Loch Ailort it is 30 miles (48km) to Strontian and 20 miles (32km) to Salen. It is also the way to Kilchoan (40 miles/64km) or Lochaline (51 miles/80km) for ferries to the Isle of Mull.

When the railway was being built Lochailort was the site of a huge camp for the navvies who worked on the track, some two thousand living here at the height of construction, and having the benefit of their own hospital.

Lochailort Inn

Originally a drover's inn, there has been a hostelry here since at least 1650, even though the road did not reach Lochailort until the early 1800's. The present inn which was rebuilt in the 1990's is much easier to reach and offers rather more modern accommodation, a cosy bar and a varied menu available all day. (The home made tomato relish, which accompanies homemade venison burgers, is to be recommended.) **Deer stalking** or **fishing** can be arranged by the hotel.

Lochailort Inn

A former landlady of the Lochailort Inn for seventeen years was Susan McCallum who died in 1890. She was so popular that her grateful nineteenth century customers, many of them railway construction workers, had a **memorial** to her erected above the road beside the railway. (Grid reference 776831.)

Inverailort House

On the A861, about half a mile (800m) from the junction with the A830, is Inverailort House. Originally built as a farm house, it was extended in 1875 to become a shooting lodge and was another establishment which served as a WWII Commando training base. A notice at the gate gives details about access to **the hills of Moidart**.

Loch Dubh

The road crosses the railway again to follow the north shore of Loch Dubh – reputed at one time to be full of giant eels. Legend tells of **The Grey Dog of Meoble** which is said to haunt this area, howling for her dead master: MacDonald of Rifern had to go away without his faithful dog. The dog pined for him and ran away, settling on an islet in Loch Dubh where she raised a litter of pups. On MacDonald's return he swam out to the island to find her but she had gone hunting and the young dogs attacked and killed MacDonald.

During the construction of the railway Loch Dubh was dammed to provide water to run a turbine to drive the rock drills, the idea supposedly having come to Robert McAlpine whilst in the dentist's chair. South west of Loch Dubh lies the wild terrain of the **Ardnish Peninsula**, where much Commando training took place.

Our Lady of The Braes

Half way up the great curve of new road which sweeps up from Loch Ailort is a

Church of Our Lady Of The Braes

large lay-by with superb views back over the loch and also of the isolated white chapel above. The church, familiar to many as one of the locations for the 1983 film "Local Hero," is the Roman Catholic Church of Our Lady of The Braes. Built here to be visible from the big house at Inverailort, it was consecrated in 1874 but services ceased in 1964.

Over the brow of the next hill is another lay-by worth lingering at for the first glimpses of **Skye, Eigg** and **Rum**. A plaque commemorating the opening of this stretch of road in March 2004 also has information regarding the distance and direction of the islands.

At the bottom of the hill Loch nan Uamh comes into view, prettily framed beneath the arches of the **Loch nan Uamh Viaduct**, another of "Concrete Bob's" elegant creations. This one, however, contains more than just the usual cement mix as during construction a horse and cart fell into the central part. As it was impossible to recover, cement was poured in and both horse and cart were preserved for eternity within the bridge.

The Loch nan Uamh Viaduct

Loch nan Uamh
Twelve miles (19km) south of Mallaig, Loch nan Uamh is extremely picturesque. Also known appropriately as "The Loch of the Caves," it is most famous for its associations with Bonnie Prince Charlie as

it is where he first stepped ashore on July 25th 1745. It was also the place from which he finally departed. On a clear day it is possible to see the islands of Eigg, Rum and Muck across the **Sound of Arisaig.**

The Prince's Cairn
After his defeat at Culloden, Bonnie Prince Charlie spent months fleeing through the Highlands. He eventually left Scottish shores for France, never to return, on September 20th 1746. He was picked

The Prince's Cairn

up by the French frigate L'Heureux from Loch nan Uamh. A cairn, signposted from the road, marks the spot from where he left. The cairn was erected in 1956 by the Forty-Five Association and the inscription is in both Gaelic and English. Parking is at a lay-by just beyond the signpost for the cairn. Information boards tell the story.

Beasdale
The prince spent almost a week sheltering in the area after Culloden, before travelling to the Outer Isles. Only then did he learn that two French ships had anchored off Arisaig so he had to return. The road through Beasdale is lovely, winding between oak, ash and silver birch trees and carpeted with wild flowers during the spring and summer.

Beasdale Station was originally a private station for the use of people at Arisaig House.

Borrodale

Bonnie Prince Charlie stayed at **Glen Borrodale House** when he first landed in Scotland. Here he wrote letters summoning clan chiefs to assemble at Glenfinnan. When he returned after Culloden the house had been burned down as a reprisal. The owner had taken refuge in a cave on the shore and Charles joined him there for a while. It is now known as **Prince Charles' Cave**. Borrodale House was later rebuilt to the same design and using much of the same stone. Opposite the entrance to the house is the start of a three and half mile (5.5 km) **footpath to Arisaig.**

A footnote to all references to Bonnie Prince Charlie and all those who helped him: There was actually a £30,000 reward for his capture but no-one betrayed him.

Arisaig

Arisaig, "the safe place," curves round the head of Loch nan Ceall ("Loch of The Churches") beneath the towering peaks of "Sgurr an Albanaich" ("Peak of the Scotsman") and Sgurr an t' Sasunnaich" ("Peak of the Englishman.") Between the two hills is the legendary place where a kelpie (a mythical water horse) lured a young girl to a watery grave. In 1746 Arisaig was the scene of a naval battle when two ships of the Royal Navy encountered two French frigates, there in support of the Jacobite cause. The French ships offloaded the gold they had brought and escaped. (For more about what happened to the gold see the section on Achnacarry.)

Arisaig was once home to a much larger community, with a population of over a thousand. However, during the nineteenth century, large numbers of people were cleared from their land to make way for sheep grazing. They were forced to

Arisaig

emigrate to Nova Scotia and the stone remains of some of their crofts can still be found.

Arisaig has been greatly improved by the building of the new road which bypasses the village. A plaque on the bridge

The Arisaig By-Pass Road

approaching the village commemorates the opening of the section between Arisaig and Morar Bridge in March 2004.

Long John Silver, the pirate in "Treasure

Island," is said to have been based on a real John Silver who was born in Arisaig in 1853. The author was Robert Louis Stevenson, son of Thomas Stevenson of the famous family of lighthouse engineers. Today Arisaig is a popular place for tourists, arriving by car, train or boat. Its sheltered harbour (once the entrance has been safely negotiated) is a popular place with people taking sailing holidays on the western coast. The innumerable sandy beaches and rock skerries also make it a favourite with canoeists and sea kayakers.

The Arisaig Hotel

Open all year, the hotel serves meals, including breakfast, to non residents as well as guests staying at the hotel. Showers are also available for non residents. At weekends during the summer there is **live music**. The adjoining **Crofters Bar** is both dog and family friendly. There is a large lounge bar and also a **children's playroom** as well as an outside eating area.

Café Rhu

Open daily in summer, this "Gastro café" has a menu which ranges from homemade broth to international cooking. There is only one sitting for evening meals so booking is necessary. Tel: 01687 450 707. Internet access available.

Convenience Store

The extremely well stocked convenience store on the main street sells newspapers, wines & spirits, a large selection of foodstuffs, bread, pies, fruit & vegetables, barbecue requisites, beach toys and much more. It is also a place to get a good cup of fresh coffee.

The Old Library

A lovely old whitewashed building with accommodation and a restaurant serving a selection of local produce imaginatively cooked. Lunches and evening meals daily Feb – Oct. Booking is advisable. Tel: 01687 450651

Post Office

As well as the usual range of postal services, there is a good selection of postcards, birthday cards, newspapers, magazines, batteries etc.

The Land, Sea & Islands Centre

Housed in a former smithy, this is an excellent community-run exhibition detailing the social and natural history of Arisaig and the surrounding area. The exhibits are presented in imaginative and lively ways, excellent for children and grown ups alike with plenty to touch and feel! Part of the display is the renovated forge from the building's former days. Opening hours vary.

SOE Memorial

During WWII Arisaig was a training centre for SOE agents (Special Operations Executive.) On the seafront stands a modern sculpture, erected in 2009, to commemorate the  *The SOE Memorial* Czech and Slovak soldiers who trained here between 1941 and 1943.

Arisaig Marine

The modern jetty and new buildings provide excellent facilities for visitors arriving by boat or, indeed, by any other means. As well as the usual range of marine facilities, there is a marine engineer on site as well as showers and a launderette for visiting sailors The café, open daily from 9.00am to 5.30pm April –

Yacht Haven

Sept, serves home baking, sandwiches, baguettes and a good range of speciality teas and coffees. The gift shop has a range of unusual and tasteful gifts, souvenirs and cards. Tel: 01687 450224.

The Small Isles Ferry

The present ferry "Shearwater" replaced a previous one of the same name which was originally a harbour defence vessel and which was used in the D Day landings. The sea at the bottom of The Sound of Sleat around the Small Isles (Eigg, Muck, Rum and Canna) is renowned for the large variety of marine wildlife, including minke whales, basking sharks, porpoises and more than one kind of dolphin.

St. Mary's RC Church

The church, which overlooks Arisaig behind the village, is large and impressive, having been built in 1874 to replace a smaller chapel when the congregation grew too large. The remains of **St. Maelrubha's Chapel** can be seen nearby in the old burial ground, where Gaelic poet **Alasdair MacDonald** is buried. A clock on the church tower commemorates him.

The Rhu of Arisaig

A narrow, twisting road leaves the village for the Rhu of Arisaig, the rocky promontory between the Sound of Arisaig and **Loch nan Ceall**. Before the coming of the railway this was the main departure point for passengers and mail for the Small Isles. The road follows the shore with stunning views of the many rock skerries, often occupied by groups of seals. Sunsets viewed from here looking towards the Isle of Skye are breathtaking.

Canoing and Sea Kayaking

Two excellent companies operate in the area: For instruction, guided expeditions etc. see www.rockhopperscotland.co.uk. For kayak and equipment hire see www.seakayakhighlands.co.uk

Arisaig to Morar Coastal Road

The new road bypasses some of Britain's most beautiful coastal scenery while the old B8008 road winds its way between

The Silver Sands of Morar

Arisaig and Morar past wonderful white sandy beaches with innumerable small inlets. Collectively the beaches are known as **The Silver Sands of Morar.** The seas are turquoise and sparkling and studded with rocks which frame views across the **Sound of Arisaig** to the **Small Isles and Skye**. The sand dunes here were one of the filming locations for "Local Hero" which starred Burt Lancaster and Fulton Mackay. In spite of several caravan and camping sites, the area retains its natural beauty. The road passes through several small settlements including **Back of Keppoch**. (Yes, that really is a place name.)

The Cnoc na Faire Hotel really does live

63

up to its Gaelic name "Hill of The View." The Art Deco style building with its outdoor seating area overlooks old croft cottages, glorious beaches and beyond to the Isle of Skye. Open all year, except for Christmas week, the hotel serves both restaurant and bar meals, the emphasis being on using Scotland's "natural larder." The menu, including breakfast, is available to non residents and can best be described as good and wholesome with an imaginative twist.

Traigh Golf Course

Located two miles (3km) north of Arisaig on the B8008 coastal road, this nine hole golf course, described as "challenging," has a truly glorious setting. Club hire available.www.traighgolf.co.uk

The large white house set back from the road is **Traigh House**, another establishment requisitioned during the war as an SOE training school for Czechoslovak soldiers. On the wall of the house is a plaque, unveiled in 2002, to commemorate those who trained there. Legend has it that in a cave nearby once lived a headless woman. Caught stealing corn from the fields, she was separated from her head by a scythe wielded by an angry laird. Thereafter she appeared every harvest time until eventually the larger part of her was banished to Skye. Her head is said to still be near the house and one day she will return to reunite it with the rest of her body.

Camusdarach

There is a camp site and car park here as well as a beautiful white sandy bay with fabulous views of Eigg and Rum. Another fine beach can be found further along the road at **Camus Aird nam Fiasgan**, the estuary of the River Morar. This is one of Britain's shortest rivers and carries water from Loch Morar to the sea in a series of dramatic waterfalls.

Morar

The main A830 bypasses the village, making it a quiet, peaceful place. It is a popular base for walkers and also with families because of its clean, safe beaches.

The Morar Cross

On a hill behind Morar is a seventeen feet (5m) high cross commemorating a visit by the Redemptionist Fathers in 1889. Morar had managed to remain a stronghold of Catholicism in spite of The Reformation and persecution. The original cross has been replaced several times over the years, the latest one having stood there since 1965. The road to the cross and viewpoint begins near the station.

Morar Station

This is the penultimate stop on the Fort William to Mallaig leg of the West Highland Railway.

The Morar Hotel

Right in the centre if the village, the family run Morar Hotel began life in 1902 as The Station Hotel and enjoys panoramic views, especially from its **Silver Sands Restaurant**. Being only three miles (5km) from the fishing port of Mallaig, freshly caught fish features daily on the restaurant menu. Bar snacks are also available. Open April – October.

Walks around Morar

There are several walks of varying lengths. An **information board** near the station gives details of some of the most popular.

Morar Motors

Filling station, breakdown and repair

service. Tel: 01687 462118

Sunset Morar Thai Food

This establishment is quite unique and provides a food experience, rather than just a takeaway meal. Genuine, fragrant, Thai food is pre-ordered from an extensive menu and cooked to individual taste by a lady chef who was born and brought up in Thailand. Her repertoire is a range of favourite recipes from her Thai family. Order any time for collection between 5pm and 10.30pm (except Mondays.) www.sunsetmorar.co.uk   Tel: 01687 462259

Loch Morar

Loch Morar is lovely. The Gaelic "Mor Dobhar" aptly translates as "Big Water" - Loch Morar, at over one thousand feet (300m) deep, is Britain's deepest inland water but is only separated from the sea by a mile (1.5km.) Legend would have us believe that it is home to Morag – a monster who appears before the death of a member of the MacDonald Clan.

A narrow, winding road runs along the northern shore for just the first three (5km) of its twelve mile (19km) length. About two miles (3km) along the road is a beautifully restored croft house which is the home of **Loch Morar Crafts**, selling a range of items including hand painted glassware. The road ends at a gated track which goes further up the loch. From there

it is possible to cut across to remote Tarbert on Loch Nevis and be picked up by boat by prior arrangement. Tel: 01687 462320.

Fishing and boat hire on Loch Morar

Brown trout, salmon, sea trout and char inhabit Loch Morar. **Fishing permits** are available from Morar Motors, Loch Morar Boat Hire or the Loch Superintendent. Mr. V. De Fresnes. Tel: 01687 462388. **Loch Morar Boat Hire.** Tel: 01687 462520

Mallaig

Mallaig is a bustling place with a busy harbour: Fishing boats large and small, as well as car ferries and private boats, all vie for space in the harbour. It is also the end of the line for the West Highland Railway and the port from which Caledonian MacBrayne operate ferries to the Isle of Skye (for the Outer Hebrides) and the Small Isles.

Until the mid nineteenth century the village was not much more than a few isolated crofts near the sea. The land here was part of Lord Lovat's estate. Tenants were moved to what is now Mallaig and persuaded to take up fishing as a means of earning a living. Mallaig grew with the arrival of the railway. This meant that fish could be transported quickly to major cities and so the industry flourished and Mallaig became one of the main ports for landing herrings. During the 1960's

Eigg and Rum from the Coastal Road

Mallaig was the busiest herring port in Europe with several smokehouses for processing herrings. Today, only one smokehouse remains although it is still a major fishing port, landing mainly haddock and shellfish. It is also an important tourist centre with all the main facilities including banks, a chemist, a filling station, newsagent, supermarket and several restaurants and cafés.

Accommodation – there is a range of hotels and guest houses in and around Mallaig, the largest being the **West**

Mallaig

Highland Hotel which sits at the top of the hill overlooking the town and enjoying excellent views. (Open Easter – October.)

Mallaig Visitor Centre
Privately owned, this is a really excellent facility with information, advice, a wide range of maps and guide books, tea, coffee and souvenirs.

Along the **main street** is a variety of **gift and souvenir shops**. In addition, **The Harbour Shop** is a well stocked newsagent selling a range of souvenirs, guide books, confectionary etc.

Restaurants
There is a wide choice of cafés and restaurants, too numerous to mention and almost all on the main street, so easily found. **Fish and Chips** are almost obligatory in Mallaig because haddock does not come fresher than here where it is landed, as is a variety of other seafood.

The Tea Garden on the main street is a good place to while away a half hour watching the World go by. Budget accommodation is available at the **Backpackers' Lodge** above the Tea Garden premises. There are several traditional bars in Mallaig, along the main street and up Davis Brae.

Mallaig Heritage Centre
Situated adjacent to the station, the interesting displays and old photographs detail the history of the area and tell the story of how Mallaig developed. Admission free. Open all year, hours vary.

Jaffy's, otherwise known as J. Lawrie & Sons, produce world famous kippers which they will pack and mail if required. A kipper is a herring which has been split and gutted before being soaked in brine and then smoked. Jaffy's kippers are smoked using the shavings from Scottish malt whisky barrels which give them a unique flavour. Jaffy's is the only remaining traditional smokehouse in Mallaig. Their shop is at the entrance to the station and also sells fresh fish and other smoked seafood.

Adjacent to the station platform is a takeaway bar serving fish and chips, tea, coffee and seafood filled rolls.

The Book Shop. Do not be deterred by the portacabin appearance: Situated half way up Davies Brae, this is a well stocked shop offering a good selection of local books and guides as well as general books.

St. Columba's Church. This is the pretty white Church of Scotland building up the hill from the main street.

The Indoor swimming pool is situated at the top of the hill overlooking the town.

Mallaig Lifeboat

When not at sea, the lifeboat can be seen in Mallaig Harbour, although it is not generally accessible to the public. It is a robust Severn Class boat, named the Henry Alston Hewat and is regularly called upon to aid stricken vessels in the sometimes turbulent waters around Skye and the Small Isles. There is an **RNLI gift shop** on the approach road to the ferry terminal.

The Mallaig Harbour Mural

Visitors to Mallaig cannot miss a spectacular Soviet style mural covering one side of the old brick smokehouse near the harbour. The piece was commissioned

Mallaig Harbour Mural

by Sir Cameron Mackintosh and The Mallaig Harbour Authority in 1998 and executed by renowned Scottish artist James McCallum. In keeping with the artist's interest in using art to explore the human condition and in particular that of working people, the mural depicts the development of Mallaig through its people – many significant events symbolically represented and cleverly interwoven.

Fisherman & Child sculpture

Another piece of public art in Mallaig is a sculpture by Mark Rogers of a fisherman and child looking out to sea from the end of the harbour breakwater.

Trips from Mallaig

MV The Grimsay Isle

A boat trip with a difference: Sea fishing and/or wildlife spotting on a traditional Scottish fishing boat, picnics onboard or ashore, catch and cook your own fish. A real fun "must do." Tel: 01687 462652. Mob: 07880 815158

Caledonian MacBrayne Ferries

Mallaig is the point of departure for Armadale on Skye, as well as The Small Isles: Rum, Muck, Eigg and Canna. Day trips are possible as well as non-landing cruises to The Small Isles.

Bruce Watt Sea Cruises

TSMV Western Isles is the vessel of Bruce Watt Sea Cruises. Operating all year round, Mon-Fri. in summer and three days weekly in winter, this is the way to travel to **Inverie** or **Tarbet** (by prior arrangement) in Loch Nevis on the remote Knoydart peninsular. This is also the way the mail travels to these two remote settlements. At Inverie is **The Old Forge,** mainland Britain's most remote pub - accessible only by boat or by a hike of almost twenty miles (32km) over the mountains. (Tel: 01687 462267.) The Bruce Watt booking office is situated at the harbour. Tel: 01687 462320

Public toilets
Glenfinnan Visitor Centre
Along the coastal road at Traigh
Mallaig Station
Mallaig sea front beyond the Visitor Centre
Internet access
Café Rhu, Arisaig.
Mallaig Visitor Centre

USEFUL INFORMATION

Telephone numbers
Police (emergency) 999 (or 112)
Fort William: 01397 702361
Mallaig: 01687 462177
Spean Bridge: 01397 712222
Fire (emergency) 999 (or 112)
Ambulance (emergency) 999 (or 112)
Coastguard (emergency) 999 (or 112)
Mountain Rescue (emergency)999 (or 112)
Hospitals
Fort William Belford H'ptl 01397 702481
NHS 24 08454 242424
Dentist
Fort William: NHS Trust Dental Services, Belford Hospital
Mallaig: Health Centre, Victoria Rd.
Pharmacy
Caol: Lloyds 01397 703403
Fort William: Boots 01397 705143
Lloyds 01397 702031
Mallaig: Village Pharmacy 01687 462209
Tourist Information Centres can be found at:
Mallaig Visitor Centre 01687 462883
VisitScotland, High Street, Fort William. 01397 701801
Bus Companies
City Link: 08705 505050
National Express: 0870 5808080
Trains
National Rail Enquiries 08457 484950
Ferry Services
Caledonian MacBrayne 01687 462463

Breakdown Recovery
Fort William (Caol), FCH Motors 01397 701515
Mallaig: Morar Motors 01687 462118
Taxis
Fort William: Numerous & readily available
Mallaig: Franco's Taxis 01687 462800
Ordnance Survey Maps
Road Map 2 Western Scotland & The Western Isles Scale: 1: 250,000
Landranger Series. Scale: 1: 50,000
41 Ben Nevis, Fort William & Glen Coe
40 Mallaig & Glenfinnan, Loch Shiel
Bibliography:
Beyond The Great Glen: F. Reid Corson
The Glory of Scotland: J.J.Bell
Lochaber, A Historical Guide: Paula Martin
Roads To the Isles: Tom Atkinson
The Weathermen of Ben Nevis 1883 - 1904: M.Roy
The Highland Hotel & Its Surroundings: Michael Wells & Chris Lumb
Iron Roads To the Isles: Michael Pearson

> The publishers would like to thank Ian Abernethy of Ben Nevis Book Corner, Fort William, for his invaluable assistance in sharing his wealth of local knowledge.

"SEE IT.... DO IT.... DON'T MISS IT !"

Visit our website:
www.scotlandguidebooks.co.uk